D0282782

DISCARDED
From Nashville Public Library

Straight Talk About Learning Disabilities

Kay Marie Porterfield

Facts On File, Inc.

For Mrs. Shepherd
and the other teachers who
refused to give up on me

Straight Talk About Learning Disabilities

Facts On File, Inc.
11 Penn Plaza
New York NY 10001

Library of Congress Cataloging-in-Publication Data

Porterfield, Kay Marie.
    Straight talk about learning disabilities / Kay Marie Porterfield.
        p.   cm.
    Includes bibliographical references (p.   ) and index.
    ISBN 0-8160-3865-1
        1. Learning disabilities. 2. Learning disabled children—
Education. I. Title.
LC4704.P67   1999
371.92′6—dc21
98-55947

Facts On File books are available at special discounts when purchased in bulk quantities for businesses, associations, institutions, or sales promotions. Please call our Special Sales Department in New York at (212) 967-8800 or (800) 322-8755.

> The advice and suggestions given in this book are not meant to replace professional medical or psychiatric care. Readers should seek professional help if they are experiencing severe emotional or behavioral problems. The author and publisher disclaim liability for any loss or risk, personal or otherwise, resulting, directly or indirectly, from the use, application, or interpretation of the contents of this book.

You can find Facts On File on the World Wide Web at
http://www.factsonfile.com

Text design by Cathy Rincon
Cover photo and design by Smart Graphics

Printed in the United States of America

MP FOF 10 9 8 7 6 5 4 3 2

This book is printed on acid-free paper.

Contents

Preface: Scatterbrain

Chalk scraping against the blackboard as I stand lecturing my college psychology students or the smell of oranges and peanut butter push memories of Mrs. Shepherd's fourth grade gifted and talented class to the front of my mind. Seeing an old school desk at a yard sale, the kind with a slanted top that swings up to reveal a compartment for books and papers, makes me recall how our desktops squeaked as we pulled out our arithmetic books to master the mysteries of long division. As those memories return, so does the sick feeling in the pit of my stomach and the tightness in my chest and throat.

I scrunched down in my seat, holding my breath and trying to make myself invisible so I would not be called on that day 40 years ago in Mrs. Shepherd's class. Throughout September I had been lucky. My teacher hadn't told me yet to join other students at the chalkboard in the front of the classroom to do math problems. I believe she thought I was painfully shy and didn't suspect my withdrawal was provoked by the fact that I hadn't a clue about division—long *or* short. I was just as ignorant about multiplication and could barely add and subtract.

From first grade on I hid the shameful secret that I had absolutely no understanding of math by trading my school lunches and occasional toys from home in exchange for answers to homework problems. A quiet little girl who gave teachers no trouble, I was rarely called on in class. Occasionally I came up with a right answer by sheer luck, but I had no idea how I had done it, just as I hadn't a clue about the series of mistakes that led me to the wrong answers. Because illness had caused me to miss many days of school, everyone assumed I'd fallen behind the rest of the class and would eventually catch up. All that changed when a family move forced me to change schools in the middle of third grade. On my first day at the new school I was given a placement test. When the half hour was up, I'd only finished four problems. Three of my answers were wrong.

As a result I was banished to a special class for slow learners. The thing I hated most was the taunts "dummy" and "retard" that came from neighbor children who passed me in the hallways. Almost as difficult to endure was the boredom of that classroom. Handed stacks of mimeographed worksheets to color, I refused to even look at the instructions printed in pale purple ink. After I'd shoved them into my desk, I wrote a 20-page novel about the Aztec. The teacher accused me of copying it from a book, but my mother came to my defense arguing that no published book could possibly contain even a small portion of the spelling errors that marked my work. Despite my failure to understand math and having a spelling system only I could decode, at the end of third grade the principal decided to place me in Mrs. Shepherd's fourth grade gifted and talented class where I sat now fighting the urge to throw up.

"Kay Marie, please go to the board and solve problem number five." Mrs. Shepherd's voice, which had sounded grandmotherly to me before, suddenly took on witchlike tones to my ears.

Somehow I made it to the front of the rows of desks, despite my wobbly knees, only to discover once I'd arrived that I'd left my math book at my seat. Everyone watched as I retrieved it and slowly copied the problem on the board, my shaking fingers barely holding the chalk. Even copying numbers at my desk seemed like a form of torture. I still wrote *6, 4,* and *7* backwards, and I confused *6* with *9* as well, since they both looked the same to me. For reasons unknown, no matter how hard I concentrated at the task, some of the numbers always took on a life of their own, breaking free from their neat rows and columns to scatter themselves across my blue-lined notebook paper. The blackboard, with its wide open spaces, only made matters worse.

As I wrote on the board, I prayed silently for the floor to open up beneath me and swallow me whole.

"Keep trying," Mrs. Shepherd urged as I wrote and erased one number after another. "You're a smart little girl. I don't know why you have such trouble with math." She went on to the next child, promising to come back to me later.

The students standing beside me solved their problems and were allowed to return to their desks while I stood in a daze, my mind filled with a jumble of meaningless numbers. I hoped against hope that Mrs. Shepherd would forget her promise.

All my life I'd heard how smart I was. That compliment always came right before the bad news that made it clear just how backward I *really* was. "You're such a smart girl, I don't know why you can't learn to tell time . . . learn the difference between *b* and *d* and *p* . . . don't know left from right . . . can't learn to write cursive. You're so scatter-brained! What's wrong with you?"

My report cards often came home with the note that I daydreamed in class and that I was an underachiever. My teachers and parents scolded me to pay attention and try harder as if I were creating the confusion that seemed to control my mind on purpose. Didn't they know I was trying as hard as I could? For the life of me I couldn't figure out why getting the right answer was so important. None of it made any sense, not the long division problem, the expectations placed on me, nor the confusion that clouded my brain. Although the slow class bored me, I believed I was stupid and that I belonged there.

The only one left standing at the blackboard, I could hear my classmates stifling giggles behind my back while I struggled to come up with an answer that would please Mrs. Shepherd, my favorite teacher. I didn't want to let her down even though I suspected my placement in her class had been a mistake.

Frustrated and overwhelmed with a sense of failure, I began crying huge wracking sobs that made my whole body shake. My wails were so loud they scared me. They must have shocked Mrs. Shepherd too because as soon as they began she let the other students out for early recess and hugged me in an attempt to calm me.

"You don't know your multiplication tables, do you, Dear?" she finally asked.

Unable to reply with words, I shook my head, certain I'd be transferred out of her class.

"Well, you've changed schools, and it's a big jump from where you were in third grade to this class," she said. "We'll just have to get you some help."

After it became clear I couldn't pull myself together, holding my hand she walked me to the nurse's office and instructed her to call my mother. Mom was angry at the scene I'd caused, but with Mrs. Shepherd's urging, she got over her embarrassment at the disgracing spectacle I'd made. Soon she and my father began working with me every night after school to help me catch up on my work.

They drilled me on math facts and spelling words, refusing to let me eat dinner until I gave them the correct answers. Most nights after dinner I spent hours hunched over my mother's old Palmer Penmanship book from her own school days, trying to imitate the flowing lines of cursive script. When I wasn't doing that, I sat across the kitchen table from my dad, who believed that by playing dominoes I might somehow catch on to the math facts that had eluded me before.

There was little time for writing poems or drawing pictures, no more chances to work on the neighborhood newspaper I had typed each week on Mom's battered Remington and sold to neighbors for a penny. From now on I had to "get my head out of the clouds" and stop being "lazy." The fact that my spelling mistakes were fewer and that I could communicate more clearly when I typed were taken as evidence of my stubborn unwillingness to learn and deliberate carelessness. Although they never said it outright, I suspected my parents took my confusion as a sign that I was a bad child. At best I was a bitter disappointment.

In self-defense I stayed up nights hidden beneath my covers with a flashlight, forcing myself to improve my reading, sometimes having to repeat one word five or six times just to make sense of it. In the end, Nancy Drew saved me, she and Laura Ingalls Wilder. Their stories pulled me through the tangled maze of letters, words, and sentences and into another world where no one accused me of not listening or not trying. They took me a step away from feeling bad about being teased for being clumsy and from feeling rejected when I was the last one to be chosen for teams in physical education. The imaginary worlds they introduced me to put not being able to figure out how to tie my shoes into perspective.

With their help I persisted through fourth grade and the rest of elementary and junior high school. On my own I learned to focus on my strengths and poke fun at my weaknesses before others had a chance to do it and hurt my feelings. Although my grades were never outstanding, I managed to get by.

Once I reached high school, through their books, John Steinbeck and Ernest Hemingway protected me from feeling too awful about my problems with Spanish, driver's education, gym, and algebra. When I came home these authors were always waiting. They, along with Rumer Godden, Flannery O'Connor, and Katherine Anne Porter, convinced me to keep trying and eventually go to college.

I wanted to tell stories as well as they did, and I knew I would need to get more education to be able to do that.

At college I gave up trying to learn what I was expected to know in conventional ways. Accepting the fact that I was different, I struck out on my own defiant course, getting through four years by making long lists of what I needed to do and taking what other people, normal people, might call short cuts. In the process I found out that knowing where to look up the right answers was more useful than trying to cram them all into my head at once anyway. Having discovered that my independent thinking was valued by some college professors, I actually liked some parts of school. I liked them so much that five years after graduation, I enrolled in graduate school.

It was there that I first heard about learning disabilities and about dyslexia, a type of learning disability that alters the way the brain processes information. Never formally diagnosed, I found I had been struggling with the symptoms since before I'd started kindergarten.

I discovered that people with dyslexia:

- reverse letters;
- have a difficult time telling right from left, which causes them problems with activities like telling time and tying bows;
- may have a hard time doing math because they reverse numbers and sometimes try to solve problems backwards; and
- tend to have above-average intelligence.

At last I had found an answer to the mystery of why a girl as smart as me could be so thickheaded. More important, I found out there are many ways people with dyslexia and other learning disabilities can make their lives easier. Some of these tricks, such as making lists, highlighting passages in books with colored markers, using a typewriter instead of writing by hand, and asking people to draw me a map when I needed directions, I'd already discovered on my own. Other tricks were new to me. I discovered the world of calculators and then computers with spell-check programs. I found out that as an adult it isn't considered cheating to trade a batch of my "killer" chocolate chip cookies with a friend in exchange for his or her proofreading services or to ask for help in other areas of my life.

The more I have come to understand the problems my dyslexia has caused me, the clearer I can see the gifts that it has given me. I focus on my strengths and find new ones. Along the way it becomes easier for me to set realistic goals for myself and achieve them. While I will probably never be an accountant or a computer programmer, I was able to complete graduate school in counseling with a straight A average. After that I began a career as a writer and have published more than 500 magazine articles and 12 books. During the past 10 years, I've also worked as a college writing teacher. Not bad for a woman who was once labeled a scatterbrain. Looking back, I now know that my learning disability didn't cause me as many problems as did the negative judgments I made about myself because of it.

Despite my successes, dyslexia still affects my life. No matter how often I practice the jokes people tell me, I still can't repeat them without getting the punch line all wrong. The thought of learning a second language scares me half to death. Even though I try my hardest to concentrate, I often forget to dot my i's and cross my t's—or I dot my t's and cross my i's. When I'm forced to give directions, I still have to reach for a pencil to know which hand is my right one. If I am tired, stressed out, or have something else on my mind, I'm likely to misspell my son's name on his birthday card, put salt in the cake instead of sugar, or stare at the grocery store shelf, bewildered at why anyone would print *APES* on a can label with a picture of peas.

Most of the time I don't let those things bother me. The fact that I can see the big picture, come up with creative new ideas, and understand that there are many right ways to do things makes me a valuable person—someone worth knowing, someone worth hiring. The fact that I have to keep my own phone number written on the first page of my address book for the times I forget it, isn't very important in the long run. Occasionally people still call me a scatterbrain, an air head, a dizzy blond, or worse because my mind works differently than theirs do. After I explain my dyslexia to them, if they persist in teasing, I avoid them at the same time I feel sorry for them. Their learning disability—intolerance—may be a far greater handicap than my own.

For a time I hated Mrs. Shepherd for uncovering my secret and for sentencing me to my parents' harsh efforts to help me pass fourth grade and every grade after that one. I disliked my mother and father even more for their nightly lessons, which I considered a torture, and for admonishing me to finish college the times I became overwhelmed and wanted to drop out. Today I know that neither my teacher nor my parents understood learning disabilities or what to do about them. Although their methods aren't the ones teachers and parents would use today, the people who cared about me did the best they could. Sensing there was hope, they refused to give up on me and they refused to let me give up on myself. For that I will always be grateful.

1

Learning Disabilities: A Hidden Problem

From the time he started school, Gary's* behavior got him in trouble. Instead of sitting at his desk and working quietly, he zipped around the room bothering other students. No matter how often teachers corrected him, within minutes Gary was off and running once more, letting the hamster out of his cage at the science center, tipping over the open jars of paint in the art corner, and making a general nuisance of himself. He wanted people, including his teachers, to like him, but he couldn't sit still or even wait his turn.

Even though he was better now, he still lost friends by cutting in front of someone in the lunch line or blurting out the answers in class after his teacher had called on another student. His head was filled with so many ideas; he *had* to get them out. He always seemed to put his foot in his mouth, saying whatever popped into his mind. It seemed

*Everyone identified by first name only in this book is a composite—a portrait drawn from details that come from many different people.

like he spent more time in the school office than in his classes. Even there he could never manage to sit still.

Wanda was lucky when her first grade class began to read. She always managed to find a place in the reading circle where she would be called on only after several of her classmates had read aloud the pages the teacher assigned. Every student was expected to do so. By the time it was her turn, Wanda had memorized the words and only pretended to look at the book.

As the years went by, Wanda learned to read quite a few words by memorizing their shape, but she couldn't sound out the letters to make good guesses at words she hadn't seen before. She hated it when her classmates laughed at the wild guesses she made when she had to read out loud in class in later grades. Their teasing made her feel so bad that she hated school and promised herself she would drop out as soon as the law allowed it.

Then she wouldn't have to put up with all the red correction marks the teachers put on her papers for messy handwriting and spelling mistakes. She wouldn't have to hear her parents warning her about how she was going to fail school or to listen to her older sister's jokes about how she must have been standing behind the door when brains were given out. She wanted to do better, but no matter how hard she tried, nothing worked. Giving up seemed like the only answer to her.

Nathan was the kind of young man who would have forgotten his head if it wasn't attached to his body, his parents said. Often it seemed to be true. Even when they or his teachers repeated the things they expected him to do and carefully explained the way they wanted them done, he would forget what they had told him five minutes later. For a while he tried to make lists of his chores around the house and his homework assignments, but then he would forget where he put them, so that strategy did him no good.

Besides, he couldn't look at lists during tests in his high school classes. To do that would be cheating.

With his poor memory, it was no wonder he didn't do well on tests in many of his classes, especially the ones in which teachers lectured most of the time. Their words literally seemed to go in one ear and out the other.

A Hidden Problem

Gary, Wanda, and Nathan all have something in common with one another. They also share an important similarity with George Washington, Thomas Edison, and Cher. They are all bright, creative people, and all of them had or have a learning disability (LD), a disorder that affects the brain's ability to understand, remember, or communicate information. People with learning disabilities have a difficult time interpreting what they see and hear or linking information stored in different parts of the brain. They may also have trouble with important skills such as

- listening
- reading
- writing
- spelling
- speaking
- coordination
- self-control
- attention

Since the symptoms of a learning disability aren't always obvious, people who see, understand, and respond to the world differently than others, don't always understand *why* they seem to be operating on a different wavelength. Many times their teachers, parents, and friends may not be aware that they have a good reason for not sitting still, having difficulty reading, or being unable to follow directions. The result is frustration on both sides. Often people like Gary, Wanda, and Nathan are criticized or made fun of because of their behavior. Driven by shame, some of them try to hide their problem. Others act as if they don't care or don't want to learn because pretending causes them fewer hurt feelings than trying their hardest only to fail.

To understand just how frustrating a learning disability can be, read the following simple passage and then answer the questions at the end. If you miss more than one question, you will fail the test.

B asketdall, the nost qop ular sport in Americatobay, was lmve ntedin 1981 b y Jamcs Naismit n, a callege qnisicaleb ucation instructor attne Imternat iomal Y ounp Men's Christia n Training School inSp ringfieldNas saehuse tts. M r. Nais mith' ssiubemts w erer o wby, dorcd, an dlazy. As wimter abbro ache b, tye teacnertri e d to tni hkof an activity to keed nisstud ents puietl y occuqiep imside tnegynna sinm. Hemabe nbt hri tee mrules, inelubi ngno ruming withe pal. Thehhe naile btowempty qeacn dasketsto tnewal lateach end oft he gyn.T he game of paskctdallw asqorn.

1. *Myova sJa mes Maisnitn?*
2. *W he rebip h etcach?*
3. *Ho ww amyrules biqth egam ehaye?*
4. *Mhe nwa spask etball inveuteb?*

You have just experienced what a person with a severe visual and spatial learning disability endures every time he or she must read something. Was this quiz easy or difficult for you? As you tried to read the material, how did you feel? If you began to get confused and angry because the words seemed to be written in some kind of senseless secret code, you aren't alone. Perhaps you felt nervous as you tried to answer the questions. No matter how hard you tried, maybe you felt that no way could you pass this test. Did you keep going or did you want to give up?

Think about how your feelings might change if you were taking this test in school and the results would affect your grade? Most classroom tests are much longer than this one. Now imagine how you would feel if everything you tried to read—from the back of a cereal box to billboards—was as difficult as this, but you had no trouble remembering and understanding what people told you or what you learned from TV. How would your life be different from how it is now?

Now read the unscrambled version of this paragraph again and take the quiz once more to see how well you do.

> *Basketball, the most popular sport in America today, was invented in 1891 by James Naismith, a college physical education instructor at the International Young Men's Christian Training School in Springfield, Massachusetts. Mr. Naismith's students were rowdy, bored, and lazy. As winter approached, the teacher tried to think of an activity to keep his students quietly occupied inside the gymnasium. He made up thirteen rules, including no running with the ball. Then he nailed two empty peach baskets to the wall of each end of the gym. The game of basketball was born.*

> *1. Who was James Naismith?*
> *2. Where did he teach?*
> *3. How many rules did the game have?*
> *4. When was basketball invented?*

Even though learning disabilities often are a hidden problem, such difficulties are common. In the past some researchers believed that only one out of 100 people had learning disabilities, but this estimate is changing. The American Academy of Child and Adolescent Psychiatry currently sets the figure at 15 percent. According to recent estimates by the National Institute of Mental Health (NIMH), as many as 15 to 20 percent of people have some form of learning disability. Some experts believe that the actual numbers are higher.

As research continues on LD, educators are aware that people with learning disabilities can succeed if they receive appropriate help. In the United States and Canada, laws have been passed requiring schools to provide this assistance. Even so, a number of students with learning disabilities do not receive the support that they need to be able to learn to their full potential. According to the U.S. Department of Education, a little more than 4 percent of all school children received special education for learning disabilities. Many adults who finished or dropped out of school before the law required public schools to diagnose and help students with LD are unaware of the reasons why they found school so difficult. Some of them remain unable to read or do math and have difficulty at work and at home because they never received the proper help.

The awareness that LD exists is fairly new. Until about 25 years ago, teachers didn't even know LD existed. They believed that students who had difficulty learning either were lazy or lacked intelligence. Since that time researchers have discovered that learning disabilities are neurological—they originate in the brain. Even though we know now that all learning disabilities are caused by a problem in the way the brain is made or how it works, not all learning disorders show themselves in the same way. Every person with LD is unique. Some people with LD have a single distinct problem that affects their comprehension, but others have several learning disabilities that overlap so that more than one area of thinking is affected. Disabilities can range in severity as well. Each one can mildly, moderately, or severely affect how a person learns.

The signals that someone might have one learning disability, or several, are many. Some people, like Gary, can't sit still and may be told they are *hyperactive* or *hyper*. As Gary does, they have short attention spans and are impulsive, acting or speaking without thinking. Others, like Wanda have a hard time reading, especially new words, and they have great difficulty spelling. Still others, like Nathan are very forgetful.

Some other signs that an otherwise normal child, young person, or adult might have a learning disability are

- performing unevenly on tests, from day to day and from subject to subject;
- struggling to follow directions;
- awkwardness;

- reading very slowly and even more slowly out loud;
- rambling on in a conversation or having a hard time coming up with words;
- often missing the point of a joke;
- a dislike of talking on the telephone;
- trouble remembering names;
- being easily frustrated;
- coming to class late or unprepared;
- being seen as immature by others;
- always wanting to do things one way;
- difficulty understanding the concept of time;
- getting lost easily; and
- disliking surprises.

Do you think you might have a learning disability? Read the following statements and see how many of them you agree with.

1. I have difficulty remembering right from left.
2. Sometimes I mix up letters and numbers, like mistaking *52* for *25* or being unable to tell the difference between *b, d, p,* and *q.*
3. I have a hard time playing sports, especially ones in which I have to catch a ball.
4. My handwriting is so sloppy even I can't read it sometimes.
5. I'm always losing things like my jacket, my lunch money, and my homework.
6. Long division and fractions are very hard for me.
7. I can't even spell *algebra,* let alone work the problems.
8. My room, my locker, my desk, and my papers are a mess.
9. I hate to read, so I don't know why I'm reading this book.
10. The only thing in life I hate more than reading is school.
11. My parents and teachers say that I don't try hard enough and have a bad attitude.

Agreeing with some of these statements does not mean for certain that you have a learning disability, but if you answered yes to more than two or three of them and you could relate to some of the LD signs discussed earlier, you might want to talk to your parents, a trusted teacher, or a school counselor about the school problems you are experiencing. Ask about the possibility of being tested for a learning disability in order to receive special help in school. We'll talk more about diagnosing learning disabilities in Chapter Three.

Not every learning problem that people have is LD. Before a student can be sure that his or her problems in the classroom are caused by a learning disability, other causes for the difficulty need to be ruled out. If a reading problem is caused by poor eyesight, then the student needs an eye examination and glasses, not special education. Some reasons for people having a hard time concentrating and remembering that are *not* learning disabilities include mental retardation, a condition of limited mental ability; poor hearing; and physical problems such as spinal cord injuries. Frequently ill children who miss a great deal of school can fall behind in their work. Students who attend school regularly but must take medication for allergies or illness, sometimes suffer side effects from the prescriptions, which make it difficult for them to achieve in school.

Some students really *are* underachievers. They don't do their homework because they'd rather be watching television or hanging out with their friends. In school, they choose not to pay attention or to put in the time and energy it takes to master the subjects being taught in their classes. Others experience major school problems because they were placed in classrooms where the work is too difficult for them to handle. Still others are a little slower than their classmates to develop thinking and motor skills because they haven't matured enough yet to be able to handle the work of a particular grade.

Emotional problems such as depression and anxiety can also make it difficult for students to concentrate and learn.

Stress from living with an alcoholic relative, divorcing parents, moving, and other major life changes can cause schoolwork to suffer too. Children and young adults who live in poverty may have difficulty paying attention in school because they are hungry or are worried about whether their family will have a place to live.

For some students English is not their primary language, the first one they learned and the language spoken at home. They may have difficulty understanding what the teacher is saying until they gain a better understanding of the language used in the classroom. Other students grow up in homes where there are few if any books, magazines, and other materials that would stimulate their curiosity and give them a chance to practice skills needed in the classroom. If their parents seldom talk with them, they may be lacking in language skills because they have not been exposed to the types of talking and listening that are part of school.

Can you come up with other reasons why a student might have problems in school?

LD—Sorting Fact from Fiction

Since the study of learning disabilities is so new, many people who aren't directly involved in education and research don't know much about LD. Believing any of the following tall tales about LD, only makes the problem seem worse than it really is.

The myth: Learning disabilities affect people only in school.

The truth: Learning disabilities affect every part of a person's life because they affect how a person perceives or interprets information and how they organize that information. In addition to schoolwork, LD can make it difficult to do activities people without learning disabilities take for granted, such as following the instructions on a box of cake mix or learning how to drive. In addition, some people with LD have problems with social skills. They may find it difficult to get along with their families or to form friendships because of some of the symptoms of their disability. Young children with LD may have problems with playing, and older people with LD sometimes find that they have to work harder to get and hold a job than people who don't have a similar condition.

The myth: Most people with LD just grow out of it.

The truth: Although learning disabilities sometimes seem to improve over time without special help, LD can be a lifelong condition, according to the National Institute of Mental Health (NIMH). Some people are able to find ways to cope with a learning disability on their own, but many adults with undiagnosed LD struggle through their lives for years believing they lack intelligence or have an emotional illness.

The myth: LD can usually be cured by taking medication.

The truth: Medication has been shown to help with the symptoms of one type of LD called attention deficit hyperactivity disorder (ADHD), a problem that makes it difficult for people to focus on one thing at a time and causes them to be so active they have difficulty learning and getting things done. Even though medication works to calm people with ADHD so that they have a chance to center their attention on the task at hand, it does not cure the LD. Instead it helps to ease the symptoms to the extent that a person can find ways to manage them.

The myth: People with learning disabilities could do better if they just tried harder.

The truth: A strong determination to succeed is an important part of coping with any problem we may face in life. If we don't put in an effort, we don't get results. Most people with learning disabilities do try very hard. Until they are diagnosed and taught strategies that help them cope with their particular LD, they often spend a great deal of time and energy trying things that don't help. Because learning disabilities cause people to think and learn differently than people who don't have them, trying to learn and to live the way everybody else does simply doesn't work. After trying and failing a number of times, some people with LD simply give up.

The myth: Because so many of them don't do well in school, people with learning disabilities must be stupid or slow.

The truth: Learning disabilities do not have anything to do with a person's basic *ability* to think and to learn, instead they affect the *ways* in which a person can and can't learn. People with learning disabilities are of average or above-average intelligence. Some studies of people with dyslexia show that the percentage of them with above average intelligence is higher than in the general population. Once people with LD receive help and learn to accommodate and work with their disabilities, they usually are just as able to learn and to achieve in life as anyone else. Many of them excel.

The myth: People with learning disabilities are losers.

The truth: Not only are people with LD just as smart as or smarter than others, they often have clusters of talents in areas like in art or music. Some people with LD seem to be more sensitive than "normal" people, and that can be a talent too. As we'll discuss later, a number of famous people who are known for their achievements in many areas of endeavor have or had LD during their lifetime. Recently some educators have come to suspect that these people have made brilliant contributions to the world because their learning disability also gave them an ability to think more creatively.

The myth: Being labeled as having a learning disability will hurt more than help a person. It is kinder to say they are "learning challenged" or that they have a "learning difference."

The truth: The term *learning disability* is the most accurate way to describe the problem. Words such as *learning challenge* and *learning difference* aren't clear because every person learns in slightly different ways from the next person and most of us find learning something a challenge. These words are imprecise and could mean nearly anything.

Many advocates for the rights of people with learning disabilities and those who work to educate people about LD believe funding for learning disabilities programs might be cut if the problem were to be given a different name. They also fear that laws protecting people with LD from discrimination in schools and the workplace might not be renewed. They feel that *learning disability* helps people to be aware of the severe difficulties LD can cause for the people who have it.

Even though a student might not like the words *learning disability,* being identified means that he or she can get the needed help to succeed in school and in life and can also be a start toward self understanding. Knowing that you have a learning disability is not half as harmful as thinking you are crazy or stupid, two words children and teenagers who have LD sometimes hear from their classmates or even insensitive adults.

Many individuals who are diagnosed with LD prefer to be called *people with learning disabilities* rather than *learning disabled.* That way of talking about it acknowledges the disability but puts the emphasis on the person not the problem.

2

LD: What It Is and Why It Happens

One of the most important things to know about learning is that most of it doesn't happen in school. In fact, we learn the most significant lessons we will ever master long before we ever step inside a school. When babies are first born they are helpless and must rely on other people to meet all of their needs. They can't sit up, stand, or move around. If they are hungry or hurt or their diaper needs changing, they can't tell anyone what is wrong and ask for what they need. All they can do to communicate is cry. That helplessness doesn't last long, though, because babies are amazing learners. Within about six months, babies figure out how to sit up. Next comes discovering how to crawl and then to stand up with support. At about one year babies can usually stand and walk with no help. Then, before you know it, babies are talking.

Just for fun ask your mom or dad if they can remember the first word or words you ever said. Chances are, you first spoke when you were between 10 and 15 months old. If you were like most babies, the very first words you said were the names of people, favorite toys, or common items around the house—things you could point to or hold in your hand. Next you probably learned some words for things that weren't physical, visible objects—words like *come* and *run* and *hungry.* Within two or three months of speaking his or her first word, a toddler starts using two-word sentences, saying things like "Get milk," or "Where toy?" As the months go by the child understands and learns how to use more and more words.

This process of learning to communicate is called language development. Language development doesn't just happen—it is learned, and it is only one of the sets of skills that babies must learn. Instead of having it easy, like many of us think they do, babies are always doing their homework. It's not easy work to do either.

All language is symbolic; the words we use stand for something else: For instance, the word *cat* stands for a furry little animal with four feet, whiskers, and a tail, but the word isn't the animal. Some words are more symbolic, or abstract, than others. You'd have a difficult time drawing pictures of words such as *to, of,* and *justice.* How do you think children learn the meaning of words abstract words like these?

Learning to speak and understand language is complex, a fact you are already aware of if you've ever tried to learn to speak a language different than the first one you learned when you were younger. In order to understand what others are saying and to speak so that others can understand what you are trying to say, some of the things you needed to know were

phonology: learning to make the sounds that make up the words of the language. (You might think your baby brothers or sisters are babbling, but they are really practicing language sounds, getting ready for the day they will say actual words.)

morphology: understanding the smallest meaningful pieces of words—morphemes—and using them correctly. (*Big* is a morpheme, so is *er.* If you put the two together, you get *bigger,* which has a different meaning than the two individual pieces.)

syntax: knowing how to string words together into sentences and phrases that make sense. (Perhaps once upon a time you said things like "Car the see," but you probably learned to say "See the car" fairly quickly, unless you have an expressive language disorder, which we'll discuss later. How do you think you learned to do that?)

Your Busy Brain

If you were like most children, your brain didn't get to take a vacation from learning after you mastered understanding and speaking. Instead you started school, where you were expected to learn to read.

Reading is a more complicated skill to master than speaking because reading takes your thoughts another step away from the concrete world of things that you can see or touch, such as cars and cats and apples. In order to read English and many other languages, you must learn how to decipher the code of written symbols called letters that stand for the sounds of spoken words. The further our thoughts move from things we can actually see or touch, the more abstract they become. When you consider that written words are symbols for spoken words, which are also symbols, you can begin to understand why some people have a very difficult time learning to read and why a few people cannot learn to read at all.

The ability to read requires doing many different things at once. After we've learned to read and can do it well, we often forget how complex this skill really is. Grab a bookmark to keep your place, then turn to a different page of this book and read a paragraph or two. As you read, try to pay attention to all the things you need to do in order to make sense of the symbols you see printed on the page. When you've finished, write down as many of those skills as you can. Then come back to this page and compare your list to the one below.

Some of the things you must do in order to read include

- opening the book, holding it still, and turning the pages, all of which require coordination of the type developmental psychologists call fine motor skills.
- moving your eyes across the page without losing your place—another fine motor skill.
- focusing your attention on printed marks and not the noise from the lawn mower outside or the student talking with the teacher in another part of the room.
- being able to distinguish one letter from another.
- recognizing the sounds that are associated with the letters your eyes see on the page.
- decoding how those sounds fit together into recognizable words.
- understanding how the words fit into sentences.
- making pictures in your mind and creating ideas.
- guessing what the words that are new to you mean from the words around them.
- comparing the new ideas you just read to what you already know.
- storing the useful ideas in your memory.
- pulling out that information when someone asks you a question about what you've just read.
- keeping track of all these processes at once and not getting confused. This ability is sometimes called *executive function*.

Since complex activities such as reading require the ability to master many tasks, the learning process can break down at a number of points along the way from start to finish. Even though someone's ability to see and to move his or her eyes across a page might be fine, perhaps that person can't form or hold mental images. Another person might be able to master everything but figuring out how to make meaning from the way words are arranged into sentences. Maybe he or she can't tell the differences between the spaces or the letters because of the way his/her brain perceives the page. Focusing might be a problem for that person—he/she just can't pay attention to printed material long enough to read it. Or, as in the reading experiment you did in the last chapter, the person might reverse many letters, which makes it hard for him or her to decode print. Or the person might have what is called a *sequencing problem,* which causes letters and words to be perceived in a different order than that in which they are printed on the page. Memory problems can make it very difficult for a child to learn the alphabet, an essential skill to master before learning to read. How many other things can you think of that might prevent a person from reading easily?

Reading isn't the only subject we are expected to learn in school, but it is one of the most basic. Students who have reading difficulties tend not to do well in other subjects. Wanda's reading problems made it almost impossible for her to make sense of the story exercises she was required to do in math. There was no way she could come up with the answer when she couldn't figure out the question.

In addition to requiring the ability to read, writing, spelling, and working math problems involve still other types of motor skills and thinking processes.

Even though Nathan could read as well as the other students in his classroom, he had poor comprehension and couldn't remember what he had read. When he tried to write compositions, his ideas raced in several directions. Forgetting what he intended to say two minutes before, he wrote anything down in order to fill his paper and get finished with the assignment. Often his teachers told him his work made no sense.

No matter what the subject, new skills are taught in each grade, building on what we were expected to learn the year before. For example, kindergartners are taught how to hold pencils and to write the letters in their names. First graders learn to print by copying letters and words, and by the end of the year they can write short stories.

In elementary school, when Gary's classmates were busy writing short reports about different animals, he struggled to hold his pencil so that he could control the direction in which it went. Sometimes it seemed like it had a life of its own. At the end of second grade, when the rest of his classmates learned cursive, or script, handwriting, his struggle became more intense. The teacher expected longer and more complex sentences. Gary couldn't produce them because he was too busy fighting with his pencil to get words in cursive down on paper. By the time his third-grade teacher began talking about punctuation and capitalization, he had given up.

By fourth grade, students write complete sentences and even paragraphs. They usually know how to choose the right word, and their punctuation skills are improving. By the end of elementary school, they are expected to write longer themes with varied sentence patterns. They've learned the parts of speech and can write sentences using correct grammar. In a few short years, most students have come a long way from holding a pencil and tracing letters. Gary, however, wasn't one of them. Believing he was stupid and angry that he couldn't keep up, he defiantly refused to write or ripped up his papers before handing them in, all the time pretending that learning wasn't important to him.

If you want to see just how much your writing skills have improved from when you started school, try this experiment. Write your name and then one or two sentences from this book with your left hand if you are right handed or with your right hand if you're left handed. Now try making up a couple of sentences on your own and writing them with that same hand. Did your hand feel tired? What about your brain? Imagine how you would feel if you had to start doing all the writing you are asked to do in school with your nondominant hand. People with certain types of learning disabilities must face that prospect every day. Learning to write as well as you can now took a great deal of concentration and the mastering of many skills.

Types of Learning Disabilities

Many learning disabilities are caused by problems in the way the brain interprets information it receives through the senses. This process is called *perception.* Although we see with our eyes and hear with our ears, smell with our noses and taste with our tongues, we perceive with our brains. Our perception can trick us into thinking things are different than they really are. Perhaps you have seen a full moon rise. Did it look huge to you when it was near the horizon where the sky meets the land, then seem to shrink as it moved higher in the sky? The moon didn't really get smaller, but if you are like most people, you perceived that it changed size.

To test how much your perception can trick you, taste a lemon. Now eat half a spoon of sugar and taste the lemon again. Which time did the lemon seem more sour? Did the lemon change, or did your perception of how it tasted change? Why do you think that happened?

As new skills are taught each year, students with undiagnosed learning disabilities who do not receive special help tend to fall further and further behind their classmates as happened to Gary, Nathan and Wanda. Since one skill builds on another, they are unable to catch up on their own.

During the years that educators and scientists have been studying the many things that can go wrong when people try to learn, they have come up with several different ways to name and classify those problems. Since we still know more about *how* LD affects learning than we do about *what*, aside from faulty perception, causes LD, the labels we use reflect the outward signs that a particular learning disability is present and not what within the brain brought it about. These names for different types of learning disabilities help experts make sure that people who have LD get exactly the help they need. One of the most commonly used systems of talking about learning disabilities is that devised by the American Psychiatriac Association.

Developmental Speech and Language Disorders

Developmental speech and language disorders are difficulties in communicating through spoken language. They interfere with the learning that must take place before a child begins school. Three forms of developmental speech and language disorders that a child can have are

Developmental Articulation Disorder. Some children with this problem have trouble controlling how fast or slowly they speak. They may speak so quickly that they slur, or run their words together, to the point that others cannot understand what they are saying. Some take much longer to learn basic speech sounds than do other children. Other children with this type of LD lisp. Instead of saying run, they might say wun or thum. Stuttering, repeating the first sound of a word over and over again, is another developmental articulation disorder.

Developmental Expressive Language Disorder. Children with this disability can correctly make the sounds that words are made up of, but they have trouble using those words. For example, a child who is four or five might still speak in two-word sentences. Another way that developmental expressive language disorders show themselves is when children use incorrect grammar long after the time other children have learned to speak grammatically. A six-year-old who says, "Me want to go home," probably has an expressive language disability.

Developmental Receptive Language Disorder. Children who have this type of learning disability often can't make sense of certain sounds, words, or sentences. For some reason having nothing to do with hearing, the sounds they perceive are jumbled. If their brains were radios, we would say they were on a different frequency and had poor reception. This problem causes them to misunderstand directions and be unable to follow them as other children can. Because we learn to speak by imitating others, people with developmental receptive language disorder often have an expressive language disability as well. When they can speak, they may ask others to repeat what's been said again and again in order to make sense of it.

Academic Skills Disorders
The second type of learning disabilities, called academic skills disorders, usually don't reveal themselves until a child is expected to master tasks such as reading, writing, and arithmetic, activities that are normally first encountered in school.

Developmental Reading Disorder. Sometimes called *dyslexia,* this learning disability affects an estimated 2 to 8 percent of elementary school children. People with dyslexia may have difficulty not only with reading but with writing and spelling as well. They have a hard time using letters to sound out words. Often they learn to read by recognizing the shape of the words instead of the letters that make them up. Many people with a developmental reading disorder reverse letters or the way letters are arranged in a word. Quite a few people with dyslexia struggle with knowing right from left, which makes it hard for them to tell time.

Sometimes people with developmental reading disorders have difficulty putting information in order and keeping it organized in their minds.

Developmental Writing Disorder. Children with this type of learning disability may find it nearly impossible to write. Sometimes their problem is the inability to write grammatical sentences. Other times, writing difficulties can come from uncoordinated hand movements and memory problems. They also may have problems with spelling. If their handwriting is extremely messy and they take a very long time to write, they are said to have *dysgraphia.*

Developmental Arithmetic Disorder. Mathematics is a very complex and abstract subject. If you listed all the things a person needs to know to do a math problem and come up with the right answer, your list would be a long one. Chances are it would include

- being able to recognize numbers and know what they stand for;
- telling the difference between +, -, and the other signs that tell you what you are supposed to do;
- memorizing addition, multiplication, subtraction, and division facts;
- being able to write numbers in their proper columns;
- knowing how to sequence (doing all the steps in their proper order); and
- understanding concepts such as place value and fractions. People with a developmental arithmetic disorder have difficulty with one or more of these abilities, resulting in problems in math. This type of learning disability is sometimes called *dyscalculia.*

Attention Disorders

Attention disorders are neurobiological conditions that can cause people difficulty in many areas of life.

Attention Deficit Disorder (ADD).   Attention deficit disorder causes people great difficulty controlling their attention. They may not be able to focus on any one thing at a time, instead paying attention to everything going on around them, or their attention may shift very rapidly. Other times they get stuck on one thing and cannot shift their focus away from it. ADD also causes difficulty in organizing the many small tasks it takes to learn and to accomplish daily activities.

Some people with ADD have a hard time figuring out which task to do first. Their inability to focus attention and to organize often leads them to make careless mistakes. Frequently they don't finish what they start, including homework and chores, and seem very forgetful. Frequently losing things and an inability to pay attention to details are also signs that a person may have ADD.

According to the National Institutes of Health, at least 20 percent of children with other learning disabilities also have ADD. Other researchers estimate the number may be higher.

Attention Deficit Hyperactivity Disorder (ADHD). Hyperactivity is a complicated way of saying that a person is much more active other people. From 3 to 5 percent of all school-age children are hyperactive, according to the American Psychiatric Association. According to researchers, as many as 15 to 20 percent of people with learning disabilities show some degree of hyperactivity.

Hyperactive people

- have a hard time sitting still;
- fidget and move around a lot, seeming to be always on the go;
- can't play quietly;
- talk too much;
- interrupt other people;
- often can't control what they say or do; and
- have difficulty taking turns.

Not long ago many learning disabilities experts believed that more boys than girls were hyperactive. Now the experts have changed their minds and think that more boys are diagnosed with the disorder because the actions of hyperactive boys tend to bother teachers more than those of girls. Why do you think this might be so?

At the beginning of Chapter One you met Gary, Nathan, and Wanda and found out about the problems they face in school. Take a few minutes to review their stories in order to refresh your memory. When you've done that, find out how much you've learned about LD. What learning disability do you think each of these young people has?

Gary's disability is fairly easy to figure out. He has ADHD. Wanda has a developmental reading disorder, or dyslexia, but her writing is affected too, so she would also be diagnosed as having a developmental writing disorder, or dysgraphia. Nathan's learning difficulties are more complicated than Wanda's. Considering that from the time he was a young child he has had a hard time following directions, he probably has a developmental receptive language disorder. He also suffers from ADD, which accounts for his memory problems. Because he can't focus his attention in order to be able to memorize, his work in English and math is affected.

If you had a difficult time with this exercise, you are in good company. Even educators and psychologists who make their livings diagnosing learning disabilities must spend many hours with each child who has a learning problem in order to figure out exactly what part of the learning process has gone wrong. They, too, struggle to sort out the many pieces of the learning disabilities puzzle for every child who is having problems at home or in school.

The biggest reason why it is so hard to sort out different kinds of learning disorders and put names to them is that they often overlap. If you have difficulty reading, for example, then you will have trouble in math too, because before you can work a problem, you need to be able to read the numbers. If you have ADD and find it nearly impossible to pay attention, then you will have difficulty in many, if not all, of your classes, since learning anything, from math to spelling, demands that you pay at least some attention to what you are doing.

Solving the LD Mystery

Although they are absolutely certain that LD has nothing to do with a person's intelligence and nothing to do with his or her character, even the experts aren't 100 percent sure why people have learning disorders. Not long ago researchers worked very hard to pinpoint a single part of the brain that was responsible for all the things that can go awry when someone tries to learn. Today most of them believe that problems originating in more than one part of the brain make it difficult for people to learn. In addition they are starting to uncover clues that there is more to LD than simply how the brain is made.

How the brain functions can also cause its owner to have learning disabilities. These disturbances in how the brain works are so subtle that they are hard to detect. Although new technology in the form of positron emission tomography and magnetic resonance imaging now allow researchers to examine workings of the living brain, much remains to be discovered before a precise understanding of the many causes of LD can be gained.

Why all the mystery? The brain is one of the most complex and amazing parts of the human body. Just consider these brain facts.

- When a baby is born his or her brain weighs only a quarter of what an adult brain weighs, but by the time the child is two, his or her brain will be 75 percent of the weight of an adult brain, which is about 3 pounds.

- Brain cells continue to develop long after an infant is born.
- An adult's brain makes up only about 2 percent of his or her body weight.
- The cerebral cortex of your brain—the surface of cerebrum, the part that looks something like a cauliflower and is responsible for most of your thinking—contains 15 million neurons, or nerve cells, per square centimeter.
- Each neuron can make from 1,000 to 10,000 connections to other neurons.
- Neurons send several hundred bits of information to other neurons each second.

Research about brain development, nevertheless, is already beginning to provide some clues to the mysteries of LD. Scientists have found that when one part of the brain develops more slowly than another—a pattern that may begin before we are born—our ability to process information will be affected. The brain stem, the part of the brain that connects the brain to the spinal column, forms soon after conception. Within three weeks, a human fetus has a recognizable brain. Later the ridge dividing the cerebrum into two halves forms. The cerebrum is the largest part of the brain responsible for perception, language, and thinking. By the time the fetus is between five to seven months old, the brain cells have specialized, and neurons grow to form networks over which information travels.

However, when the left hemisphere of the cerebrum does not keep pace with the right side, which then must do more work than it is designed to do, a person's language skills, memory, ability to understand, logic, and ability to analyze are all affected. People who are right-brain dominant tend to take a global approach to learning and to everyday life. They have problems breaking big chunks of information into pieces or taking small steps to get a big job done. Generally they learn to read later than other children because they have difficulty decoding words by breaking them into smaller chunks.

In the opposite case, when the right side of the brain develops more slowly than the left, a person tends to have trouble sequencing or putting things in order according to time. For instance, he or she might have difficulty understanding concepts like *first, next,* and *last.* Lack of body awareness can cause a person who is left-brain dominant to appear clumsy. They may also have problems with spatial orientation. Figuring out where objects are placed or determining the background from the foreground can be very hard for them to do. Visual perception problems may be present too. Although they focus on details, many times they miss the main point. You could say that they can't see the forest for the trees.

The frontal lobes of the brain's cerebrum are responsible for carrying out what scientists who study the brain call *executive function.* Much like an executive manages all the departments and employees of a large corporation, the frontal lobes determine how the different parts of the cerebrum will interact. They direct the flow of information from one side of the brain to the other. It is also their job to organize, plan, make judgments, focus attention, and organize and evaluate information. Researchers have found that poor blood flow to the frontal lobes can affect executive function.

It is easy to see how any one of these three brain development patterns could contribute to a learning disability. Currently neuroscientists are trying to determine why one part of a person's brain would develop more quickly or work harder than another part. One theory is that the underactive part of a person's brain may not be getting enough glucose, or blood sugar. Glucose is the fuel that keeps the brain working somewhat like gasoline keeps a car engine going.

Other researchers have found that a neurochemical imbalance—too much or too little of the substances the body produces to help move information between one brain cell and another—may also contribute to LD. They have discovered that people with attention deficit hyperactivity disorder tend not to produce enough of a brain chemical called catecholamine, a substance that controls motor behavior and motivation. Drugs that increase the level of catecholamines in the brain—including dopamine, which is sometimes prescribed for people with Parkinson's disease—have been found to decrease the symptoms of hyperactivity.

Another interesting discovery is that 60 percent of children with learning disabilities have at least one close relative who also has a learning disability. One study of children with reading disabilities found that 88 percent had family members with language processing problems. Many researchers believe LD may be inherited, and they are trying to isolate the gene that might be responsible for disabilities that are passed down in families from generation to generation.

Although scientists are still trying to figure out the exact mechanics of what causes learning disabilities, they do know some things that can damage the brain's structure. The physical harm caused by these events may be only slight, but even so it can be enough to cause a learning disability.

Errors in Fetal Brain Development

During the time it is forming and growing inside the mother, a human fetus is vulnerable to harm from many different things. Some of the following conditions might not directly damage a fetus's brain but do raise the risk of premature birth, and the incidence of brain damage is higher among babies who are born early. Some of those factors that can affect the brains of unborn children include

maternal malnutrition. An unborn baby depends on what its mother eats for survival. Mothers who do not eat enough of the right kind of food tend to give birth to babies of low birthweight and who have birth defects including brain damage. Folic acid, a nutrient found in spinach, is especially important to the proper development of a baby's brain.

pregnancy complications. Intrauterine bleeding or the poor attachment of the placenta, the saclike membrane that contains the fetus and the fluid that surrounds it, can cause brain damage.

maternal diseases. Measles, toxoplasmosis (an illness pregnant women can catch from cats who eat raw meat), and sexually transmitted diseases such as syphilis can also cause problems for the fetus's developing brain. If the mother has diabetes or kidney disease, these conditions can affect the baby as well.

Rh incompatability. Sometimes a mother's blood contains a protein, Rh, that the fetus's does not. In such a case, she is said to be Rh+, and her baby is Rh-. When this happens, the mother's blood attacks her unborn infant's blood so that it is unable to carry oxygen to the fetus's brain. Lack of oxygen can cause brain damage and future learning disabilities.

poisons. Although radiation, strong chemicals, and air and water pollution definitely have an impact on the development of unborn children, the most damage is done by toxic substances, or poisons, the mother takes into her body and which pass directly to the fetus. These include tobacco, drugs, and alcohol.

Fetal Alcohol Syndrome and Fetal Alcohol Effect

Fetal alcohol effect, or FAE, is the name of a condition caused when a pregnant woman's unborn child is affected by the alcohol she drinks. When the baby is severely affected, he or she is said to suffer from fetal alcohol syndrome, or FAS. Children with FAS have below-average intelligence; those with FAE do not have as much brain damage, so their intelligence may be normal. Most have some form of learning disability.

Some of the characteristics of FAS/FAE children that affect their learning are

- hyperactivity
- difficulty focusing attention
- impulsiveness
- poor communication skills
- lack of judgment

Alcohol is the leading cause of birth defects in the United States and Canada. These lifelong problems could all be prevented if pregnant women, or women who thought they might become pregnant, did not drink. Since an unborn child's brain develops the entire time before birth, there is no safe time for a pregnant woman to drink.

Gary's mother often wonders if the fact that she drank alcohol when she was pregnant with her son is the cause of his difficulties now. She liked to party when she was younger and can remember at least two times she drank enough to become intoxicated after she got pregnant but before she realized that she was. Once she suspected she might be carrying a child and the pregnancy test confirmed it, she followed her doctor's advice and stopped using alcohol until after Gary was born. Not until her son began showing problems in school did she really understand that alcohol, even in small amounts, can cause severe damage to an unborn child's developing brain. Even though she did not intentionally set out to hurt her son, she feels like she made a big mistake that cannot be undone. The guilt she feels about it is hard for her to live with.

Brain Damage After Birth

Even after a child is born, events can still occur that damage his or her brain and bring about a learning disability. Birth itself may cause problems in a child's later efforts to learn. Long and difficult deliveries, including breech births in which the baby is born bottom or feet first rather than head first, cut down on oxygen supply to the infant's brain and increase the chances of damage that may lead to LD. The same holds true for babies born with the mother's umbilical cord wrapped around their necks. Births during which the doctor must use forceps to help pull the infant from the mother's birth canal also present an abnormally high risk for LD since a baby's brain can be damaged by forceps.

During the first year of a child's life, his or her brain continues to develop. Throughout that time a child is especially susceptible to being permanently damaged by eating lead or cadmium, usually from old paint chips. High fevers, suffocation, diseases that involve the brain, such as meningitis, and head injuries could also cause LD in an infant.

Although scientists aren't certain precisely what parts of the brain and which brain functions are responsible for all of the possible types of learning disabilities, awareness of the known causes of LD is critical for prevention. No miracle cure has been invented for learning disabilities, but with each year more is known about how the human brain thinks and what can be done to help it work more effectively. Even though many pieces of the LD puzzle remain unsolved, we do know that when people with LD receive the help they need, they can succeed both in school and in life.

3

The Emotional Impact of Learning Disabilities

Despite the As on his science lab projects that proved Nathan was a bright young man, much of the time he thought he was dumb because he did so poorly in most of his other work. School was such a struggle for Wanda that many days she felt like giving up. Even though Gary acted as if he didn't care about not fitting in, deep inside he felt like an outsider. Because of his learning disability he believed that he would always walk through the world as a stranger, almost as if he had been born on another planet. Even though they spent only about six hours a day, five days a week in school, with two-and-a-half months of vacation in the summer, the difficult times these three students had in the classroom colored their notion of who they were twenty-four hours a day, every single day of the year.

Self-esteem, the image we carry about ourselves, has much to do with whether we are winners or losers in life. Positive self-esteem, along with a willingness to work hard to meet challenges, is key to doing anything well. When we feel good about ourselves, we have a can-do attitude. When we don't like ourselves, often we don't try to do many new things because we are afraid we will fail.

Many students with LD have low self-esteem. Like Gary, Wanda, and Nathan, they have difficulty with some things that other students easily accomplish. Some are criticized by parents and teachers and teased by classmates for their inability to keep up with other students. They have been urged to try harder, when no matter how much effort they put into their schoolwork, they simply cannot learn the way everyone else does. It is no wonder they don't feel good about who they are. Learning disabilities can make life outside school difficult as well.

Nathan tries to help around the house, but he often forgets to take out the trash even when he's staring right at it. Because his mother doesn't fully understand the memory difficulties he has, she feels frustrated about always having to remind him to do things when his much younger brothers and sisters remember on their own. "You're irresponsible," she says, and he is starting to believe it.

Wanda's room is always a mess. She tries to keep it neat, but her shoes and CDs, her stuffed animals and her clothes seem to have a will of their own—just like the letters on the page when she tries to read. Every month or so, her mother tidies up for her and hollers at her all the time she's doing it, accusing her of not caring about her belongings. "If you can't take care of your clothes, then maybe we shouldn't buy you any more," she warns.

Wanda could straighten up her room if someone took the time to show her how to work on one small part at a time so as not to become overwhelmed, but she doesn't know that. Nobody has thought to teach her because people without learning disabilities often assume tasks that are easy for them should be simple for everyone else as well. Even though she goes to a special classroom at her school several times a week for help with the subjects she is taking, she isn't receiving the help she needs at home. She's starting to feel that there's much more wrong with her than the dyslexia she has been diagnosed as having. Sometimes she feels like she is retarded.

Often it seems to Gary that most of the people he knows can't stand to be around him—not even his parents. For as long as he can remember, most of the conversations he's had with them have consisted of his mother and father telling him not to do something. He knows too that he has disappointed his dad the times his father has tried to show him how to change the oil in the family car and when he has taken him fishing. In the first instance Gary tipped over the pan of old oil, spilling it all over the driveway. The fishing trip was a disaster after he got a fishhook caught in his hand and fell out of the canoe, tipping it over and dumping his dad in the lake in the process. "Why can't you be like other kids?" he was scolded.

Gary wonders that too. He would like to be like other kids his age. He'd be the happiest person in the world if his classmates would stop teasing him and ignoring him when he tries to sit by them in the lunchroom. He's tired of being called a klutz and a loudmouth and of having people tell him he's like a big baby. Sometimes he gets so mad at his family and the people at school, he's scared by the intensity of that feeling. When he's an adult, he promises himself at those times, he's going get revenge on all the people who have picked on him throughout his life.

The struggles that these young people face aren't unique to them. They stem from the fact that learning disabilities affect every part of a person's life. They also arise from another difficult fact about LD: Most people in the world don't understand that a person who has LD may not be able to meet their expectations. Accustomed to failures and hearing negative comments about themselves, like Gary, Wanda, and Nathan, teenagers with learning disabilities may decide that not only do they make too many mistakes, but they are big mistakes.

In a 1997 survey of adults with LD conducted by the University of Kansas, the people the researchers interviewed said that the most important skills they reported needing to learn weren't how to read a dictionary or find the square root of numbers. They were

- self-confidence
- effective communication
- decision making
- making friends
- getting along with family and others in close relationships

These are abilities important to a well-adjusted life. Many people who have learning disabilities lack them, but with the right type of coaching, these skills can be learned by anyone—whether they have LD or not.

I'm No Dummy

Labels can be useful tools. For example, if after being tested you are labeled as having a learning disability, that tag legally entitles you to help in school. You may receive special tutoring or be given learning materials slightly different than those designed for people without LD. When it comes time to take a test, your teacher may place you in a room by yourself so that you will not be distracted by other students. If you find it almost impossible to write, you may be allowed to speak your answers into a tape recorder.

The label *learning disability* also means that you are protected against discrimination under federal law.

You already know that learning disabilities have nothing to do with a person's general intelligence. In fact, someone labeled *learning disabled* can only be of average or above-average intelligence. You can be a genius and have LD, but you can't be LD and below average in intelligence. (Someone who has difficulty learning because their ability is below average is called *intellectually impaired.*) Even though people with LD are as bright as or brighter than other people, sometimes those around them don't understand that. Out of ignorance they might make up their own labels for a person who has LD. Just a few of these are

- underachiever
- lazy
- careless
- unmotivated
- troublemaker
- space cadet
- dumb or stupid
- crazy

The problem with these labels is their inaccuracy. After we hear them for a while, we start to believe them despite evidence that they are not true. In time we add them to the picture we carry about ourselves, and we start to act as if they were true. If people tell us we aren't smart and treat us as though we are incapable of learning, then guess what? You're right! We don't learn. This is called a self-fulfilling prophesy.

Soon it doesn't matter if other people call us names or not because we start to call ourselves names. Instead of being realistic about our learning disabilities and trying to deal with them, we blame ourselves for all the times we failed the expectations of others and our own expectations. We feel ashamed, not only of the times we have failed both inside and outside the classroom, but of ourselves as well. The situation is often made harder to bear if a person with a learning disability comes from a family of high achievers. They feel hurt when they compare themselves to other family members with many accomplishments and believe that they don't measure up to the family's standards.

Just like spelling, fractions, and the state capitals, helplessness is something we learn. Some people with learning disabilities are masters at the art of helplessness. According to Dr. Xavier Castellanos of the National Institute of Mental Health, all children have a normal drive to learn and to master the world. "When they become discouraged and become convinced that they will not be able to succeed," he says, "they detach and appear lazy." When they give up, something mental health professionals call *learned helplessness,* they feel even worse about themselves. For some young adults, giving up can mean not trying in school. Some even drop out. In a national study of students with learning disabilities conducted in 1991, 35 percent of students with LD dropped out of high school.

Young people who feel powerless to cope with a learning disability may not try other things that they want to do, such as learning how to rock climb, taking art lessons, joining clubs, or trying to make and keep friends. They also can become the target of even more criticism from parents, teachers, and classmates. Learned helplessness, the belief that there isn't any use in trying, keeps them from finding ways to stick up for themselves.

Low self-esteem is no fun. None of us want to walk around convinced we are terrible because of something about ourselves that we can't make go away. To be ashamed of ourselves is one of the most uncomfortable feelings we can experience. When we can't stand ourselves, we often try to pretend we don't feel what we're feeling. Then we look outside for ways to try to boost our self-esteem. The worse we feel about ourselves, the more important it becomes for us to have other people like us. When we feel ashamed of ourselves, the negative comments other people might make about us have more power to hurt us.

Children, teenagers, and adults with learning disabilities who feel ashamed of themselves have many ways of coping with the painful feeling of shame. Some of them try to hide their learning disability. They push themselves, working twice as hard as their classmates in order to cover up any sign that would indicate they are different from the rest. Often they are so anxious that people will find out the truth about them that they fear and avoid getting too close to people.

In the end, their learning disability may catch up to them anyway. Even working three or four times as hard as other people won't make a learning disability vanish. In fact, putting themselves under that much stress can lead to other problems that frustrate them so that they give up trying altogether.

Sometimes parents who suspect that a child has a learning disability play this cover-up game too. As long as their son or daughter makes fairly acceptable grades and doesn't get into trouble at school, they are reluctant to face the fact that the child or young person has LD. They may even help their child hide the learning problem by doing their homework for them and blaming teachers or other factors for their child's difficulty learning. When parents have difficulty accepting a child for who he or she is, the result for a child can be lowered self-esteem. Without help, people with low self-esteem can sink into depression, which may cause them to think that life is no longer worth living. Studies show that people with learning disabilities have a greater risk of suicide than those who don't have LD.

The first time Wanda's teacher told her parents about special help that she could receive, they turned it down. "There's nothing wrong with her," Wanda's mother told the school. "She just needs to apply herself." Like many who lack knowledge about learning disabilities, Wanda's parents took the teacher's comments as an insult. They thought she was telling them that their daughter was less intelligent than other students. As a result, Wanda didn't get special help for two more years. During that time she fell further and further behind and felt worse and worse about herself.

In addition to trying to act perfect, children, young adults, and grown-ups have other ways of defending themselves from the feelings of failure and being different that a learning disability can sometimes cause. One way is to feel angry. When people feel anger but either can't or won't talk about it, they tend to act it out. Their attempts to appear tough are often a way to show the world that they don't care about not living up to the expectations others have for them. According to a 1977 study conducted by the National Center for State Courts and the Educational Testing Service, 50 percent of all juvenile delinquents tested were found to have previously undetected learning disabilities. Since that time, findings from a number of other studies have consistently shown the rate of learning disabilities among juvenile offenders and adult prisoners to be between 30 and 50 percent. Today many educational psychologists consider LD, especially ADHD, to be a risk factor for juvenile delinquency.

Most people with learning disabilities don't act out in such a dramatic manner, and not all of them are angry. Many find yet other ways of trying to prevent other people from finding out they have LD. These include

- acting silly;
- being super-helpful;
- becoming a con artist about why they didn't do their homework;
- pretending to the world that they don't care about succeeding;
- acting as if everything bores them;
- blaming other people for the bad things that happen in their life;

- manipulating other people into doing things for them; and
- withdrawing to the point of trying to be invisible.

Some other young people try to escape the difficult consequences of their learning disabilities by using alcohol and drugs.

Gary started drinking after school with one or two neighborhood boys during middle school. After he drank a few beers that the boys took from their parent's refrigerator, he didn't feel so different from the other kids. They were all acting goofy, so who cared? Besides everybody seemed to think he was a bad kid, so maybe he would just prove them right.

Gary isn't alone. According to studies conducted at Columbia University, children who have been diagnosed with attention deficit hyperactivity disorder tend to have a greater risk of alcohol and drug abuse when they enter their teenage years than do students without the disorder. Their risk for substance abuse, although not so high in adulthood, was still greater than that for adults without learning disabilities. The problem with these ways of trying to cope with LD is that they don't make the original problem better. Ignoring a learning disability doesn't make it go away, and even though acting out, always telling jokes, or being a manipulator may make a person feel better for a while, they do nothing to raise self-esteem in the long run. Self-acceptance and talking about the difficult feelings learning disabilities cause, can help young people with LD find the strength and courage to begin solving their problems.

Nobody Understands Me

In addition to chronic school failure, children and young adults with learning disabilities often face rejection from others their own age. In a study done by the University of

Kansas Institute for Research in Learning Disabilities, people with learning disabilities said that after education, the area of their lives that gave them the biggest problem was their social life.

Everybody needs to feel like they belong in a family and in other social groups. Learning to get along with other people and making, as well as keeping, friends is a big part of life. As children grow into young adulthood, forming relationships and wanting to fit in become even more important. According to a study by Barker & Wright, children who are two years old and are raised in their own homes spend about 10 percent of their day playing with other children. By the time children are between 7 and 11 years old, they spend more than 40 percent of the time they are awake playing and talking with friends.

Take a few minutes to think of all of the times you interacted with people so far today. Interacting can mean talking to someone, doing something with them, or even just nodding or smiling at someone as you pass in the hallway. How big of a role do social interactions play in your life?

Harry Stack Sullivan, a well-known psychologist who studied the important role that friends play in helping young people develop into adulthood and shaping their sense of well-being, believed that friendships do many positive things for teenagers including filling their needs for

- tenderness and secure attachment
- playful companionship
- social acceptance
- emotional intimacy
- sexual relationships

When young teenagers don't get the chance to form friendships in early adolescence, their self-esteem suffers. Later on other problems can come from trying to establish dating relationships.

Teasing is one of the main reasons why young people with learning disabilities may have a difficult time getting along socially. Wanda hated it when other kids called her dumb, and she dealt with it by withdrawing and trying to avoid being around them. Sometimes when she was at home and alone in her room, she would cry about the names other kids had called her. Nathan got along with the other students at school most of the time, but when he tried something and failed, they always made fun of him, so mostly he retreated into television and later, when his folks got him a computer, he spent hours surfing the Net. Those activities seemed safer than being around people. Gary blew up at being called a "sped" (Special Ed kid) and a klutz, and he got into fistfights when people put him down.

Teasing is serious business. Sometimes it can become, not only verbally, but physically abusive. In the summer of 1998 four teenage boys in Toledo, Ohio, were accused of torturing a 15-year-old learning disabled boy with a broomstick, a flyswatter, and a belt. The attack included both beating and sexual abuse. After they were arrested, they were charged with felonious assault and kidnapping. Fortunately most incidents of taunting only leave emotional scars, but emotional abuse can have lasting results and it happens frequently.

According to a study conducted by the University of Kansas, students who have learning disabilities are often treated poorly by classmates in groups in which students were expected to work together on projects. Cooperation is a complex social skill difficult for some students with learning disabilities to master. Researchers also found that in regular classrooms, students with learning disabilities were ignored, teased, and complained about to the teacher by their peers. The good news from the study was that after the students with LD were taught how to cooperate, they did better in group work. As a result, the other students stopped teasing them.

Not all adolescents with learning disabilities become isolated and feel lonely like Wanda did. Other teenagers with learning disabilities are very social. Much depends on the type and the severity of the LD they have. According to results of the University of Kansas survey, students with learning disabilities talk with just as many other students as those without learning disabilities do. They told the researchers that they started slightly more conversations and spent more time hanging out with their friends after school and at home than students without learning disabilities did. They also reported talking on the phone as often and having the same number of close friends as other students did. The researchers concluded that students with mild learning disabilities may learn to rely on social skills to compensate for problems they have in their schoolwork.

Talking to other students in school and hanging out with them are fairly simple social activities. The University of Kansas researchers found that students diagnosed with a learning disability went fewer places with friends and invited them to activities less often. These are more complex activities and require more social skills. Teenagers with learning disabilities also took part in fewer sporting events and extracurricular activities than did teens who didn't have a learning disability.

Some other complex social skills that give some people with LD difficulty are

- persuasion
- negotiation
- responding to peer pressure
- giving and accepting criticism
- relating to people in groups
- dating

Why do you think these activities might be harder for someone with a learning disability than for a person who doesn't have one? Even though, at first glance, convincing a friend to do something may seem simple, it is intricate and requires many of the same skills, such as choosing the right words and paying attention, that are needed for classroom learning.

Consider for a moment all the bits and pieces that go into asking a friend to loan you five dollars. First you need to be aware of what kind of a mood your friend is in at the moment so that you can pick the right time to bring up the subject. While you're doing that, you need to think of a good reason—one he or she will accept—why that person should lend you the money. For that, you need the ability to put yourself in his or her shoes and be able to think the same way. When we develop the ability to look at the world from another's perspective, our dealings with others go more smoothly.

While you're planning how to borrow the money, it might be a good idea to come up with one or two more reasons in case the first one doesn't work. Then, as you are talking with your friend, you must make sure your tone of voice, as well as the look on your face, is convincing. In order to increase your chances of getting the loan, you need to be aware of the other person's words and his or her facial expression and tone of voice too in order to figure out exactly what he or she means. Such nonverbal cues are critical to understanding and communicating with other people. (According to researcher Marshall Duke, a child psychologist at Emory University, only 7 percent of our meaning is communicated through words; 92 percent is conveyed through tone of voice, facial expressions, ges-tures, and body language.) Finally, you must respond to your friend appropriately, choosing just the right words.

Sometimes students with LD have a more difficult time with complex social activities because they are slower in their social development than other children and teenagers are. Even though they are told to act their age, like Gary and Nathan they frequently seem to act younger. For this reason, some young people with learning disabilities get along better with kids who are not as old as they are. The researchers of the University of Kansas study found that three-fourths of the children they observed who had learning disabilities tended to use significantly fewer nonverbal and verbal social skills than their same-age peers. Someone with a learning disability might stare at people or avoid making eye contact with them altogether. They may stand too close to people and cause them to feel uncomfortable or touch people who do not want to be touched, either slapping them playfully on the back or giving them a hug. Difficulty figuring out what other people are feeling by reading gestures or facial expressions, like a frown or narrowed eyes, or a person's tone of voice, means that children and young people with learning disabilities are sometimes thought to be rude, insensitive, or disinterested by other people. Even though people with LD don't mean to be impolite and aren't aware that others interpret their behavior that way, many times others get angry at them.

Knowing the appropriate way to act and being able to interpret the social cues that other people give us is a set of skills psychologists call *social cognition.* In order to master social cognition, we not only need to know how to read people's expressions, the gestures they make with their hands and their voice tone, we also need to know to apply these social cues appropriately to the different people and situations in our lives. If one of your schoolmates who has always been pleasant to you before bumps into you so hard you drop your books while classes are changing and the hall is packed with students, that means one thing. If the school bully who is always threatening to hurt you bumps into you so hard you drop your books when the hallway is so empty that there's plenty of room to walk, that means another thing. If the bully is in an obvious hurry and isn't paying attention to where he is walking, it could mean yet another thing. How you interpret the cues will determine whether you respond to being bumped in an appropriate way or one that gets you into trouble.

To understand just how complex social cognition can be, imagine how a conversation might go if you were talking about your day at school to one of your friends. Now imagine having a similar conversation with the school principal who passes you in the hallway, your elderly grandmother who is dying from a terminal illness, or a future boss interviewing you for a job. How would your conversations differ with each of these people? How would they be alike?

According to a 1983 study of popular children in school done by Hartup, classmates say they like best those children who give out reinforcements like smiles and compliments, listen carefully, maintain open lines of communication with peers, are happy, like themselves, show enthusiasm and concern for others, and are self-confident without being conceited. That's a tall order for someone with a severe learning disability to fill. When you can't find the right words, it is hard to give people compliments or to make small talk. Some teens with LD, like Nathan, give classmates negative reinforcements because they don't think before they speak and instead blurt out anything that comes to mind.

Still other symptoms of learning disabilities can make it difficult for people to grasp social skills and use them. For example, Nathan didn't remember the way to a new friend's house, so he didn't show up Saturday afternoon to go to the mall with him. Instead, he spent hours wandering around. He didn't think to ask for the friend's number and he didn't think to go to the mall and wait for his friend there. The other boy was irritated at him for not keeping his word. Many other young people with LD have a hard time using problem-solving skills. They leap to a solution that doesn't work or give up entirely.

The awkwardness that some learning disabilities may cause can be another roadblock to interacting with others. For boys, who generally face expectations from those around them that they will be good at sports, this can be an especially tough challenge. One University of California study of sixth graders showed that nearly half of the boys' activities centered around sports. The girls told researchers that about a quarter of their activities had to do with sports.

Ever since he could remember, Nathan loved basketball. As a young child, he enjoyed watching games on TV with his dad and knew the names of the players on his favorite NBA teams before he had memorized his own address and phone number. His room was decorated with basketball posters, and whenever he could, he liked to shoot hoops in his driveway, dreaming of what it would be like to be a professional player.

By the time he reached middle school, Nathan was tall enough to make the team and was good at shooting baskets alone in the driveway. No matter how much he loved basketball and wanted to play it, however, when it went beyond aiming for the hoop, he tripped over his own feet and couldn't keep track of all the things he needed to remember to play the real game. His clumsiness resulted in teasing when he tried to join in pickup games at a nearby park. Since he knew he could never make the team and would be teased mercilessly if he showed his face at tryouts, he didn't go, not even to watch most of his friends who were trying out.

They made the team and were so busy with practice that he hardly ever saw them after school. When he did, all they wanted to talk about was the team. Feeling like an outsider, like a loser, was no fun, so he avoided them. Later, when his school played games against other schools, he stayed home.

People with a learning disability may have just as difficult a time figuring out their own feelings as they do those of others. Low impulse control can cause people with LD to laugh at the wrong times. Sometimes they don't laugh at jokes at all because they don't get what's funny. They may have difficulty judging the timing and rhythm of conversations, butting in or carrying on one-sided conversations. People with ADHD may talk too loudly and be too boisterous.

Other learning disability symptoms that can make it difficult to relate are

- experiencing extreme mood swings;
- having difficulty making decisions;
- not thinking about consequences before doing something;
- having difficulty reasoning;
- having a hard time adapting to new situations;
- becoming easily frustrated;
- feeling overwhelmed; or
- forgetting to bathe and wear clean clothes.

Problems getting along with others can also occur in relationships with parents. When they believe that a child or a young person is not paying attention, ignoring them, or forgetting things deliberately, parents often react with anger. Because children with learning disabilities were often "difficult babies" who cried more than other children and who did not smile when their parents played with them, the parents' exasperation may have built up over the years. It can come out later in the form of accusations and threats or sometimes violence. If one of the parents has a substance abuse problem or the family is severely troubled in some other way, the child or young person with LD may become a scapegoat and take the blame for everything that is wrong with the family and the individual family members. Sometimes educators and psychologists recommend that in addition to making sure a child receives help for his or her learning problem, the family receive counseling as well.

Other parents feel sorry for a child with learning disabilities. They do things for the child that he or she could do for him/herself and shelter their LD child from the world. As a result their children with learning disabilities may learn to be helpless more quickly and fall into that habit more deeply than children whose parents coach them to cope with their disabilities so that they can be independent.

Although Wanda's mom gets frustrated with her daughter, she makes many decisions for Wanda, such as what clothes to wear and how to spend her free time, that Wanda should be making for herself. When Wanda was nine years old and still couldn't manage to tie bows, her mother continued to tie her shoes for her instead of buying her shoes that buckled or slipped on. Sometimes she tied her shoes in front of Wanda's friends, which embarrassed her daughter. She worries when Wanda spends the night at a friend's house and is stricter with her daughter than most parents are. Wanda believes her mom tries to shelter her because she's not confident that Wanda's decisions will be sound ones. As a result, Wanda's learning disability has taken on a central role in her life, and her own confidence is dwindling. She wishes her mother would let her try to solve at least some of her problems on her own.

Although young people, both with and without learning disabilities, need parents to take care of them in many ways, they must also must start learning to take responsibility for themselves. Overprotective parents like Wanda's mom can make life difficult for teenagers, especially if they give their child with LD more attention than they do their other children. The jealousies that arise from impartial treatment cause strain on the family.

Sometimes the social awkwardness that accompanies many types of learning disabilities is outgrown over time. Sometimes it is not. Children and young people who have learning disabilities that affect their social relationships can master the skills they need if they are taught effectively. Before that can happen, parents, teachers, and the child or young adult all have to recognize that a learning disability is present. Then they can work together to help raise the self-esteem of the person with LD so he or she can succeed socially as well as in academic subjects.

4

Diagnosis and Treatment

Even though a child's learning disability itself does not worsen, school and emotional problems resulting from it pile on top of one another until someone suspects LD is present and takes steps to deal with it. The American Academy of Child and Adolescent Psychiatry calls the pileup problem of getting further and further behind in school and feeling worse and worse about oneself a "snowballing" effect. Early diagnosis is very important in order to spare a child with a learning disability unnecessary difficulties.

Once parents or teachers recognize the signs of a learning disability, the child can be tested, given the proper diagnosis, and start receiving the help that he or she needs. With the right teaching methods and coaching of social skills, people with LD can learn ways to compensate for it. In addition, changes can be made at school and at home to make life easier for the person with the learning problem. These changes are called *accommodations.*

Sometimes parents begin to suspect their child might have LD when he or she is late in passing certain developmental milestones. Other parents grow concerned at their child's activity level. Most toddlers are very active, but those with ADHD run and climb nearly all the time and are impossible to settle down. Other times it is the family doctor who notices the signs of a learning disability when parents take a child for a checkup.

Some of the signals that a young child could have a learning disability are

- beginning to speak later than other children;
- having difficulty saying words;
- being slow to learn words;
- difficulty learning the days of the week, the ABCs, and counting;
- having trouble understanding simple concepts having to do with time, such as today, tomorrow and yesterday; and
- being unable to follow simple directions.

It is very important to keep a watch for these symptoms if there is a history of learning disabilities in the family.

Quite often parents don't notice LD signs before a child starts school. If the boy or girl is their first child, they don't have a basis for comparison. Other parents suspect that their child is acting somewhat differently than other children, but they believe the child is just a bit slow to develop in some areas and will outgrow the problems and catch up with his or her peers if they are patient. They may choose not to focus on teaching the alphabet or having a child learn to write his or her name, preferring to wait until the child begins school because they don't want to push him or her too far too fast. Since children with learning disabilities are just as intelligent as anyone else, the LD may not be that noticeable until a child begins school. This is especially true if the learning disability is a mild one.

More often than not, teachers are the first to recognize that a child has a learning disability because they are in charge of teaching more complex skills such as reading, writing, and arithmetic calculation, the things that usually give children with LD the most problems. In addition to trouble with schoolwork, some things that cause teachers to suspect the presence of LD are the following:

- performing poorly on tests as compared to class partici-pation and homework;
- having a hard time finishing work in the given time;
- getting confused by the teacher's instructions;
- having difficulty getting organized;
- showing a big difference between ability to do the work and the actual end result;
- complaining that the work is too hard;
- complaining of boredom; and
- developing an intense dislike of school.

Even in the elementary grades, a child's problems can remain unnoticed, especially if the young student is a quiet one. If a student doesn't cause behavior problems in class and can do the work, even if it takes him/her longer than other students to finish it, the learning disability may not catch the teacher's attention. Teachers may believe that the child is daydreaming or lazy.

Usually the first students to be tested for LD in schools are those who are hyperactive and cause disturbances in the classroom. It was Gary's fourth-grade teacher who suggested to his parents that he might be hyperactive and that he should be evaluated for ADHD. The teacher explained that unless they could pinpoint the reason for his inability to concentrate or sit still, he couldn't get the help he needed. Not only would he continue to do poorly in school, but his relationships with other children would suffer as well.

Academic expectations for middle and high school students are much more demanding than those placed on children in elementary school. Besides not having recess anymore, young people are expected to do more reading and solve tougher math problems. They are also expected to research and write longer papers. They must learn to take notes, do more studying on their own, and take responsibility for organizing their time.

For Nathan high school was a nightmare. Because of his pleasant personality, his elementary and middle school teachers had let his difficulty following directions and remembering things slip by. When he goofed up, he'd make a joke about himself, and pretty soon he'd have them laughing too. The charm never failed—he'd always get a second chance, and sometimes a third one, to correct his mistakes. Besides, he'd become an expert at cheating. It was easy to write down the things he remembered on little slips of paper and hide them where he could sneak a peek at them during a test. It was simple enough, too, to look at a neighbor's test paper when the teacher had his or her back turned. He must have been good at it, because he never got caught.

He should have known high school would be different that first day when he got lost and couldn't find three of his classes. The year went downhill from there. The work in his new school confused him, and it was now harder to talk the teachers into allowing him extensions on his homework. Being given assignments a week or two before they were due and being expected to manage his time in order to do them drove him up the wall. "You're in high school now," they'd tell him when he asked for extra time. He knew it and he hated it. There was too much to remember. Getting caught cheating in civics class was the last straw. Luckily for him, the assistant principal looked over his school records and test scores. Although he was put in detention, he wasn't kicked out of school. Instead the assistant principal and a counselor talked his parents into having him evaluated for a learning disability.

For years Gary had wondered what was wrong with him before it was suggested he be evaluated for LD. Unfortunately his experience is not uncommon. According to a 1994 survey by the national Learning Disability Association, about a sixth of its members were diagnosed with learning disabilities as teenagers. Half of the people who responded were not diagnosed with an LD until they were 20 years old or older. Some of them had gone through school before federal laws mandated testing students suspected of having learning disabilities and providing educational opportunities appropriate to their needs. Others were educated after the laws were passed, but because their problems were not extremely obvious or disruptive, no one noticed the difficulty they were having or connected it to a learning disability.

Statistics from a 1992 study of adult literacy conducted by the U.S. Department of Education show that 21 to 23 percent of American adults either cannot read at all or have such poor reading skills that they have a difficult time filling out job applications, writing business letters, and following written directions. Although some of these adults speak English as a second language or come from other countries where they might not have received adequate schooling and others have physical disabilities such a poor vision that prevent them from reading, experts believe that many others have undiagnosed learning disabilities. While some illiterate adults are able to hold well-paying jobs, others either cannot find work or are stuck in jobs that pay very little. Today many adult literacy programs throughout the country, not only help people to learn to read, but can help adults discover if they have a learning disability as well as helping them figure out what to do about it.

Assessment: One, Two, Three Testing . . .

Finding out whether or not someone has a learning disability and then determining what kind he or she has is not a simple process. Usually an LD evaluation is done by a multidisciplinary team of educators, learning specialists, psychologists, and social workers. Sometimes physicians called neurologists—specialists in how the human brain and nervous system work—are called in to provide more detailed information. The process may take weeks to finish, but in the end the person with LD will be able to receive the specialized help needed in order to begin learning to his or her potential.

While many adults who wonder whether or not they have LD often must pay for an evaluation, children and young adults who attend public elementary and secondary schools are entitled to a free LD evaluation if they qualify under the guidelines set forth in the Individuals with Disabilities Education Act (IDEA), a law requiring schools to provide free public education for all students with disabilities. We'll be talking more about the rights this law guarantees students with learning disabilities in the next chapter.

An LD evaluation is designed to find out if the student really is achieving in school at a lower level than would be expected for his or her age. The process also determines if there is a major difference between intellectual ability and achievement in the areas of speaking, reading, reading or listening comprehension, writing, and calculating or reasoning in math. Because different states define this difference, or discrepancy, in varying ways, the diagnosis of learning disability depends to some degree on where a student lives. If these criteria are met, the evaluation team still must rule out the possibility that visual, aural (having to do with hearing), or motor handicaps are the source of a student's learning problems. Mental retardation, emotional disturbance, and other factors such as being raised to speak a language other than English or growing up in poverty must also be eliminated as the main factors causing the trouble with schoolwork.

Over the several weeks during which the LD evaluation takes place, the team will

- examine the student's school records to compare test scores and grades and to see how much school the child has missed in order to rule out absenteeism as a possible cause of the current difficulties.
- look at the teaching methods and material covered to see if a student wasn't placed in the wrong classroom.
- talk with parents to compile a medical and social history centering on the student's development. (Sometimes a doctor will do a medical examination of the child checking for hearing loss from ear infections and other problems that might cause the same symptoms as LD.)
- observe the child in classes at school and, if needed, at home.
- give the student intelligence and achievement tests. (Sometimes a psychologist will administer an individual IQ test, requiring the student to answer questions out loud and to solve puzzles instead of giving a pencil-and-paper test.)
- administer more specialized tests that can uncover which areas of information processing may be affected by the learning disability. (Like the individual IQ test, usually these involve more activities than reading questions and answering them on paper. Depending on the suspected learning disability, these tests might be given by a speech therapist, a hearing specialist—*audiologist*—or a learning specialist.)
- possibly experiment to find the ways that the student learns best by changing the classroom environment, the way the information to be learned is presented, or other factors that could affect how a student learns. (If the

student's learning difficulties can be resolved with a few minor changes in the classroom, the student will probably not be labeled as learning disabled.)

Because an LD evaluation takes up so much time and requires students to do things that may be difficult for them, it isn't always a very easy or fun process. When Wanda's sixth-grade teacher recommended that she be evaluated and her parents finally agreed, at first she was scared. Maybe the testing would prove something she'd secretly suspected for years—that she was retarded. Besides, she found it embarrassing to be called out of the classroom. The learning specialist and the school psychologist asked so many questions that she felt like she was being studied under a microscope. She put up with it because she was tired of being behind in her work and of all the teasing. If she did what they asked of her, maybe they could find out what was wrong, and better still, maybe it could be fixed.

IEP—Planning for Success

After collecting all of this information and sifting through it, the team decides if the student has a learning disability. If the answer is yes, then they are required by the IDEA law to write an Individualized Education Plan, or IEP, for the student. The IEP, which is a legal document, sets out the plans the school has to help a student with learning disabilities receive an education that is equal to that of other students in the school system. It lists the skills that students like Gary, Nathan, and Wanda need to develop in order to improve their performance in school. The IEP also lists learning activities that will help teach them these skills.

The IEP that was eventually written for Wanda, stated that she needed to be taught reading and writing skills in ways that made use of her hands, such as tracing letters on sandpaper. It was also suggested in her IEP that while she received this special help in reading and writing, she be allowed to speak the answers to her homework into a tape recorder instead of struggling to write them for hours on end. As well, the IEP maintained that Wanda needed someone to read assignments in literature, social studies, and science to her so that she could keep up with the class. She liked that idea since she had always done well in those subjects when she wasn't expected to read or write.

Usually a student's Individualized Education Plan includes

- **special services** the student might need and ideas for how the school plans to provide them. (Some special services might include sessions with a hearing or speech therapist, psychological counseling, or special tutoring.)
- **what type of classes** the student will attend. IDEA says that children must be in the least restrictive environment necessary. For most students diagnosed with a learning disability that means being *mainstreamed,* or remaining in a regular class for all or most of the day. Although some students with LD attend special classes several hours a week, unless the learning handicap is extremely severe, they are not assigned to a special education classroom.
- **accommodations, or techniques, and materials** that allow LD students to do schoolwork with greater effectiveness. Some of the accommodations that a student who has been diagnosed with a learning disability might be given are a longer time to complete tests or the use of a calculator or tape recorder.
- **changes to a child's program.** The team may decide to modify some of the requirements for a student, such as having him or her take fewer classes or substituting one class for another.

- **academic and behavioral goals** for the following year. These are listed as specific objectives, such as reading at a fourth-grade level, demonstrating an understanding of fractions or showing the ability to focus on a task for 15 minutes, that the student is expected to accomplish. Whether or not the child meets these goals is a way of measuring the student's progress and the success of the IEP plan.

When the plan has been written, the evaluation team meets with the parents and sometimes the student, if he or she is old enough, to discuss what has been discovered about the learning disability. At this time they also explain in detail the steps the school will take in order to provide what they consider the best education for that person. If the parents agree with the IEP, it will be put in place. If they disagree about how the school plans to educate their child, they can challenge the school. In the latter case the matter is usually settled in a due-process hearing explained in more detail in the next chapter.

Medication That Can Help

Even though many learning disabilities are thought to have a physical basis in the brain, there is no magical pill that a person can take to cure his or her LD. Medication does work, however, in treating some of the symptoms of attention deficit hyperactivity disorder. Sometimes the school's learning disability evaluation team suggests a student be given a prescription for medicine to calm him or her down. Other times it is the parents who seek medical help from a physician to lower the activity of a hyper child. Not only children take this type of medication. According to the National Institute of Mental Health, 80 percent of the children who take prescription drugs for ADHD remain on medication during their teenage years. Half of them continue taking the drugs as adults.

Three drugs that stimulate the central nervous system are the most commonly prescribed for hyperactivity. They are

- methyphenidate, known under the brand name Ritalin
- dexotroamphetamine, brand name Dexedrine
- pemoline, brand name Cylert

According to the National Institute on Mental Health, 9 out of 10 hyperactive children show improvement after taking one of these three drugs, which help them to focus and do better in school. Sometimes the medications improve physical coordination so that a child can write or catch a ball better. Research shows that in some cases the drugs help hyperactive people who take them slow down enough to think before they speak or act.

At first it doesn't make sense that taking a stimulant, a drug that gives most people an extra boost of energy, would work to quiet a person who already has too much energy. These three medications all boost levels in the brain of dopamine, a neurochemical, or hormonelike substance that helps carry messages through the brain. Scientists believe that too little dopamine may be responsible for ADHD.

In addition to being a central nervous system stimulant, Ritalin increases the body's production of dopamine. Because it is a powerful stimulant, doctors usually start out by prescribing it in low doses taken three times a day. Then they frequently check up on the patient to see how he or she is doing on the drug. Some of the side effects of Ritalin are stomachaches, headaches, poor appetite, and sleeping problems.

Dexedrine raises dopamine levels in the brain by blocking reuptake, the absorption of the chemical by a peron's system. Dexedrine is less expensive than Ritalin, but it has more severe side effects, including slowing a child's growth. When the young person stops taking Dexedrine, normal growth patterns return. For this reason, some physicians recommend that children take breaks from their medication. The effects of both Ritalin and Dexedrine last from three to four hours with a single dose.

Cylert's effects last from 5 to 10 hours after a single dose. One pill taken in the morning will help the child throughout the school day. Often this drug must be taken for three to four weeks before a child's symptoms of hyperactivity decrease. Cylert's side effects are the same as those of Ritalin and Dexedrine. In addition, it can cause liver damage.

Because these three stimulants are strong medications, most doctors are very careful about prescribing them. At the same time that they may decrease hyperactivity, they can worsen the tics, or small muscle spasms, called Tourette's syndrome, that sometimes accompany ADHD. Ritalin, Dexedrine, and Cylert can also cause addiction in adults and adolescents who abuse them. Children who take prescribed doses of the medication do not become addicted, according to the National Institute of Mental Health.

Clondine, or catepres, a new medication given for high blood pressure, has gained popularity as a treatment for hyperactivity and is believed to act in much the same way as the aforementioned stimulants. Nonaddicting, it can be administered through a skin patch and has been shown to decrease hyperactivity symptoms by 60 percent in those who have taken it. Clondine lessens the tics of Tourette's syndrome, but it can worsen depression in people who already show symptoms of that emotional illness.

Currently medical researchers are studying whether drugs normally used for compulsivity disorders and anxiety might decrease hyperactivity. Arthur Walters and Steven Kugler, neurologists at the Robert Wood Johnson Medical School in New Jersey, have found that L-dopa and pergolide, two drugs given to Parkinson's disease patients to increase the levels of dopamine in their brains, show promise for treating hyperactivity as well. While treating a sleep disorder with the drugs, they found that the medication helped children be more attentive, calmer, and more sociable. Although the research on this treatment is very new, it is exciting because these two drugs do not have the side effects or the addiction potential of the stimulants.

Other medical treatments for ADHD increase the level of two different neurotransmitters in the brain—norepinephrine and serotonin. Medications called tricyclic antidepressants boost the production of these two neurochemicals. These antidepressants are not addicting. Although they help level out mood swings and temper, they do not have much effect on concentration. Side effects include sleepiness, dizziness, dry mouth, and constipation. MAO inhibitors, which are also commonly used to treat depression, slow down the action of monoamine oxidase, the enzyme that the body produces to break down norepinephrine and serotonin. Although not as effective as the stimulant drugs, they seem to work better in treating ADHD than tricyclic antidepressants do.

Some people strongly believe that hyperactive children should not be given drugs to control their symptoms. They feel that the risk of side effects, such as slowed growth, are too high a price to pay for peace and quiet in the classroom. People who question the practice of prescribing medications to children with ADHD also argue that not all children who are given the drugs really suffer from the disorder. Instead their restlessness and inability to concentrate may come from problems at home, allergies, or emotional problems. Those who argue for drug therapy for attention deficit hyperactivity disorder counter that no child should have to suffer the frustration that an inability to concentrate can cause or the low self-esteem that results from teachers', parents', and classmates' reactions to behavior beyond the control of a child. Parents who are uncertain whether or not their child should take stimulants or other medications to treat hyperactivity need to talk with the child's physician and possibly get a second opinion from another doctor in order to make the best decision for their child.

Other Treatments

Parents whose children have learning disabilities, as well as adults who are frustrated by the roadblocks LD has put in their life, are often desperate to find help for their problems. Over the years many theories about why people are hyper and what should be done about it have emerged. Despite all the media coverage about hyperactivity cures, most of these treatments have not been shown to work.

In the 1970s Dr. Benjamin Feingold, an allergist from San Francisco, said he believed that artificial coloring in foods, as well as artificial flavorings and preservatives, made children hyperactive. He prescribed diets for his young patients that contained none of these chemicals. In addition he had them stop eating foods that contain natural chemicals called salicytes—foods such as tomatoes, berries, apples, cucumbers, and almonds. According to Dr. Feingold, half of his patients improved.

When the National Nutrition Foundation tested what came to be known as the Feingold Diet, however, it did not come up with results that supported those findings. In 1980, after tests on about 200 subjects, the agency concluded that the diet did not have any effect on learning or hyperactivity. The researchers stated that they believed that the few children in the study who improved slightly had done so because of the placebo effect and the fact that they had received increased attention because of the study. In 1982 a 13-member panel of experts convened by the National Institutes of Health agreed that research did not prove Dr. Feingold's treatment worked.

Often when people, especially young children, start acting hyper they're said to have a "sugar high" from eating too much candy or drinking too many soft drinks. Even though eating too much sugar isn't a good idea because it satisfies hunger without providing the nutrients that other foods do, too much sugar has not been proven to make people hyperactive. In 1984 the American Medical Association held a special meeting to examine the link between sugar and hyperactivity. The studies presented at that gathering showed no support for the link. In 1986 the United States Food and Drug Administration's Sugar Taskforce also concluded that there was no evidence to support the theory that sugar is to blame for an abundance of uncontrollable energy. Research on artificial sweeteners such as aspartame or saccharin showed no proof that they caused hyperactivity either.

Because of the difficulties that learning disabilities can cause, a number of other treatments have been advertised as sure cures for LD. These include megavitamins, eyeglasses with colored lenses, and chiropractic manipulation. According to the National Institutes of Health, none of these has been proven effective.

New forms of treatment for LD that some researchers believe hold promise are biofeedback and video games. Biofeedback involves receiving constant information about the brain waves, or electrical energy patterns, a person emits. Depending on whether a person is calm or stressed, brain wave patterns change. During a biofeedback session the individual is wired to a machine that provides feedback and is given suggestions by a technician on how to control the waves his or her brain is emitting. In the past the technique was used to help people relax and as a way to help treat stress-related illnesses.

Within the last decade biofeedback has been used experimentally to treat ADHD and other learning disabilities. Although the research on biofeedback as an LD treatment has been on a small scale, there are some indications that learning to control one's brain waves may help a person to focus attention and thereby learn better.

Researchers at Rutgers University are studying the possibility that children with dyslexia and who have a difficult time connecting sounds to letters and putting letters together to form words may benefit from playing video games. Animal researchers have found that some specially designed games can change the electrical energy patterns of monkeys' brains. These patterns, which are caused by neurochemicals and which make up what we call brain waves, may be responsible for dyslexia, the researchers believe. After playing the games, which help them tell one sound from another, children in the Rutgers study, sponsored by the Charles A. Dana Foundation, showed improvement in their schoolwork. Researchers call these new games "aerobics for the brain."

In addition to medication and other treatments aimed at specific learning problems, other help is available for people who have LD.

Social skills training teaches children, young people, and adults how to overcome some of the social handicaps discussed in the last chapter such as the inability to interpret people's gestures, tone of voice, or facial expressions. Social skills classes can also help teach children and young adults with LD how to handle teasing.

Behavior therapy, which is sometimes called cognitive therapy, helps people to change the way they act. A person with a learning disability might go to a behavior therapist to learn to think before he or she speaks, to set goals, or to stop procrastinating. Behaviors are changed by rewarding successes.

Psychotherapy helps people change the way they feel. As discussed earlier, learning disabilities can cause people to experience a number of negative emotions. People who have LD can learn to feel better about themselves and their relationships with other people by talking their problems out with a therapist. They can also learn to use techniques such as "positive self-talk," or giving themselves compliments to raise their self-esteem.

Support groups are made up of people who share similar problems. Because they've had many of the same experiences as other members of the group, they understand each other without having to go into long explanations as they would with someone who had only read about learning disabilities in a book or magazine article. Group members give each other encouragement and can share ideas that have worked for them to cope with living with a learning disability. Support groups exist for parents as well.

Classes for parents, offered by private learning consultants, mental health agencies, or schools, show them how to help their children who have learning disabilities, not only in school, but with daily living skills. Often these classes offer suggestions about how to solve family problems that arise when a child has LD. In addition parents learn to work through their own feelings about the learning disability and the child who has LD.

As awareness of learning disabilities has grown, the number of private LD consultants or coaches has increased dramatically. Many of these people are qualified and offer good assistance at a reasonable fee. Others take advantage of the hopelessness and frustration people with learning disabilities and parents with children who have LD often feel. Their presence has increased, especially on the Internet, where to open a private practice one needs only to construct a web page. Parents and students should check out alternatives before giving money to someone who claims that he or she can "cure" learning disabilities.

Local school districts sometimes offer classes or support groups as well as free counseling for students and parents. The school district's learning specialist or psychologist can help parents and young adults find other useful resources within the community. In addition, several national organizations that educate people about learning disabilities can refer people to qualified LD helpers throughout the country. They are listed in the resource section at the end of this book.

5

Learning
Disability Rights

Before the current awareness about learning disabilities, many students with LD either weren't offered help in school or the help they were given was not the right kind. For example, a bright student with a visual perceptual disorder might have been taken out of regular classes and put in a special education classroom composed mainly of students who were much less intelligent. There they might have spent the day learning colors, reading from first- or second-grade readers, and working on the simplest of basic living skills. Or a student with attention deficit hyperactivity disorder might have been given Ritalin to calm his/her behavior, but nothing was changed in the classroom to better help the student learn.

Once educational researchers began finding out more about LD, improvements started being made in the way people with learning disabilities were taught. These still didn't occur in every classroom or in every school. Some regular classroom teachers lacked the training necessary to spot learning disabilities their students had and didn't know how to teach these students. Others knew a little about LD but didn't want to change the way they were used to teaching. Some felt that it was not their job to help students with LD in their classroom. They believed that teaching those students was the responsibility of special education teachers. In some schools, especially small ones, special education departments were tiny and not designed to help students with LD. Sometimes school districts with no special education facilities would turn students with LD away, refusing to enroll them.

As a result many students with learning disabilities, students who could have learned what was expected in school if the proper teaching methods had been used, fell through the cracks. Sometimes they stayed in the classroom and were given "social promotions" being passed from grade to grade, even though they hadn't learned the skills taught that year. By the time they reached high school, they were so far behind that many of them simply dropped out as soon as they could. Others graduated with a regular diploma but could not read or do basic math skills. Without these basics, they had difficulty getting jobs and certainly couldn't go on to take further training.

That sad situation began to change in 1975 when the U.S. Congress passed a law called the Education of All Handicapped Children Act, requiring schools to provide education for students with disabilities. In addition to disabilities such as visual and hearing impairments, mental retardation, and motor impairments, the law required schools to provide a free and appropriate education for students with LD and to offer programs for them that would meet their special needs. In addition the bill provided federal funding to schools so that the provisions of the law could be carried out. Today students with learning disabilities make up half of the 5 million students in public schools covered under the law. In 1998 the United States appropriated $4.9 billion for special education.

The Education of All Handicapped Children Act recognized that students with specific needs could be taught at home, in hospitals, and in special education classrooms. However, it required public school districts to educate the students residing in their boundaries in the least restrictive environment possible. The law viewed special education, not as a place, but as a collection of services provided to a child. For most students, that resulted in mainstreaming—being placed in a regular classroom and receiving special accommodations in the classroom and academic support. Today most schools provide mainstreaming for special education students with learning disabilities, pulling them out of the classroom for one or two hours a day to work with teachers who have been trained in LD teaching methods. These teachers are known as learning specialists. Recently the federal government has encouraged schools to place learning disabled students in the regular classrooms even further by allowing school districts to spend special education money for special learning tools, such as computers and software, even if they will be used by all students in the classroom.

I've Got a Bright IDEA

In 1990, when the Education of All Handicapped Children Act was renewed, it was renamed the Individuals with Disabilities Education Act, or IDEA. Its official name is Public Law 101–476. Because this law protects students who for the most part are still minors, rights are granted to their parents. Most elementary school children aren't interested in laws and, because they are so young, might not be able to make wise decisions about their educations. By the time a student is in high school, though, chances are that he or she is more aware of his or her rights and wants to have more say in how he or she is educated. Although a high school student with a learning disability who is still a minor cannot challenge the school if he or she believes that appropriate services aren't being delivered, a young person can become aware of the law and ask his or her parents or guardians to question the school or request hearings to resolve the problem if necessary. For that reason it is important for teenagers with learning disabilities to understand the law.

The basic rights of parents with children ages 3 to 21 who have LD include the following:

- a free education that meets the needs of toddlers, children, and young people with learning disabilities
- placement of the child in the least restrictive setting possible, one that will provide the most contact with students who do not have disabilities
- notification by the school whenever it decides to evaluate a child or change the child's placement
- ability to request an evaluation from the school if they believe their child has a learning disability
- testing of the child in the language in which he or she is most fluent
- participation in the development of the child's Individualized Education Plan
- agreement in writing to the results of the evaluation and the school's IEP for the child before the plan can be put into place (Parents can withdraw their agreement at any time and can request an independent evaluation that the school must consider in making a decision about how best to teach the child.)
- ability to request a reevaluation when it seems to them that their child's placement isn't working out well (According to the law, a reevaluation must be done automatically every three years.)
- review of all of the child's school records and ability to request that mistakes be corrected (If the school doesn't comply a parent can request voluntary mediation or a court hearing to resolve the issue.)

- updates of their child's progress in school at least as often as parents of students without disabilities are informed of their children's progress
- ability to request a due-process hearing from the school to settle differences that can't be talked out informally. If that doesn't work, the parent can request mediation or a hearing before a judge

The earlier learning disabilities are diagnosed and addressed, the greater are the chances that a child will be able to do well in school and in life later on. For this reason, the law ensures the rights of infants and preschool children participating in government-funded early childhood education programs. During the 1993–1994 school year 154 infants and toddlers with disabilities received help under IDEA. Instead of receiving an Individualized Education Plan of the sort we discussed in the last chapter, children who are too young for school receive what is called an Individualized Family Service Plan, or IFSP. The IFSP usually focuses on services that can be provided in the home.

Canadian laws that ensure the rights of students with learning disabilities to an education vary from province to province. On the whole, however, they are very similar to the U.S. law, including the same type of evaluation and individual education plans.

In addition to providing preschool services and services for students while they are in school, IDEA requires that IEPs detail the plan of the school district to prepare students to adjust to life outside the classroom when they leave high school. According to the 1997 amendments to IDEA, transition planning must begin when the student is 14 years old to allow enough time to explore future careers and to provide activities that will help him/her get ready for life after high school.

Like the IEP, transition planning is done in a way that will meet the needs of the individual student. All transition planning is done by a team made up of school personnel, members of the agencies or schools that will help the student after graduation, and parents. Unlike IEP meetings, the student attends transition planning meetings. Because transition planning is aimed at helping the student to be more independent, he or she is expected to participate in the process of planning his or her own future. For the transition plan to work best, the student with learning disabilities needs to pay attention to what the other members of the team are saying and to speak out about what he/she wants and needs instead of sitting silently in the meeting and letting the adults make all the decisions.

The activities recommended include instruction, community experiences, and goal setting. For example, one student might be expected to spend some time with the school counselor, taking aptitude and interest tests and working on developing a resume. Another student might be advised to sign up for a work/study class. Part of another student's transition plan might be to take vocational training in high school or prepare to take it afterward. When necessary, life skills are also taught. If the student plans to attend college, the transition planning will help him or her get ready for that too. More information about career choices and college is discussed in a later chapter.

Because Nathan's learning disability was not diagnosed until after he had begun high school, transition planning for him began shortly after his Individualized Education Plan was put into place. When he was asked to attend his first transition planning meeting, he was unsure about what to say. He still didn't know much about learning disabilities, so he decided it would be best to let the experts make the decisions for him. When the school district's LD specialist asked him about his career goals, he couldn't come up with an answer, because he rarely thought about the future. Just getting through the day was difficult enough.

As the school psychologist, his teachers, and the learning specialist talked, Nathan remembered how much he had wanted to be on the basketball team two years before. After he'd realized that his dreams were unrealistic because he lacked the coordination to make them come true, he'd given up. He'd given up on dreams for the future altogether.

The guidance counselor asked him again what he wanted to do with his life.

"Something to do with basketball," he said and wished he could disappear as soon as those words came from his mouth. They were going to tell him it was a dumb idea; he just knew it.

To his surprise the members of the transition planning team didn't. Instead they began discussing the number of behind-the-scenes people required to do all the jobs pro basketball created: advertising people, office workers, employees to order and take care of the uniforms and the equipment, trainers. By the time five minutes had passed, he realized that running a pro sports team was a business and that all kinds of people were needed to make sure it ran smoothly. Maybe there was a place in basketball for him.

As the planning continued, the team members began suggesting the steps he needed to take to find out more about job opportunities and about his own skills. He was glad he'd taken the risk of telling them what was on his mind.

Some of the ways in which students can participate fully in planning the future are to

- understand the learning disability they have, including how it affects learning and might affect work
- give careful thought to what they would like to be doing in the future and set realistic goals—not ones that are too high to achieve or ones that are based on low self-esteem rather than on what the students really can do
- begin exploring possible careers and learning what education or training is necessary in order to do that type of work

- start building a personal file that includes academic records a copy of the IEP, a résumé, and some samples of schoolwork
- begin becoming familiar with their rights as people with learning disabilities
- find out about resources that provide help for people with learning disabilities and take responsibility for finding and contacting those that could provide assistance
- work on developing both academic skills and social skills

Under IDEA if parents do not want their child evaluated for a learning disability, then the child cannot be evaluated by the school, as happened when Wanda's parents refused her teachers' suggestions. Sometimes after a child has been evaluated, his or her parents don't agree with the team's diagnosis or the Individualized Education Plan. They may not want the child to attend special classes or to receive accommodations recommended in the plan. If parents refuse to sign the IEP, then it will not be put into place and the child will continue to attend regular classes.

More often, parents may refuse to sign an IEP because they believe the school will not provide enough help for their child. If they don't agree with the educational plan and cannot reach an agreeable solution to the conflict with other members of the IEP team, under the law, they have a right to ask for mediation before a fair and impartial professional mediator. The mediator hears both sides of the issue and comes up with recommendations. If mediation fails to get both parents and the school district to come to an agreement on how a child with LD should be taught, then parents can take the school district to court and have a judge decide whether the proposed IEP will meet their child's needs.

When Gary was first diagnosed with ADHD in eighth grade, his mother and father didn't believe that the Individualized Education Plan the school's team had devised for him provided enough help. The school agreed to provide tutoring, but his parents felt he needed more specialized instruction since he was so far behind on his work. Although his intelligence was well above average, he read at the fourth-grade level and his math skills were those of a fifth grader.

His parents agreed with the part of the IEP that suggested their son begin taking medication to improve his concentration, but they wanted him to spend the school year in a special classroom where he could get more individual attention. They believed that would give him a better opportunity to catch up and have a fresh start when he began high school. Administrators told them that what they requested was impossible since the special education classroom was overcrowded.

When Gary's mom refused to sign the IEP, she asked that the conflict be resolved in mediation. The mediator agreed that Gary needed more help. He also agreed with the school that there was no room for Gary in the special education classroom. He told the family that Gary needed to continue attending regular classes at least part of the day, but he worked with the school to revise the plan so that Gary would be transported to special classes at another school building in the district each morning. Once his work was at the eighth-grade level, he would return to the regular classroom for full days and have access to tutoring when it was needed. It was a plan everyone could live with.

Should the school staff refuse to do an evaluation because they do not suspect that a child has a learning disability, the student's parents can have one privately done. This allows them to select who will be on the team that assesses their child. In this case they, not the school district, are responsible for paying for the evaluation. Schools are not legally required to make changes in a student's education based on the information provided in a private LD evaluation, however, parents can take the school district to court to give a judge the opportunity to decide if the school district should provide special services for the student and pay for the evaluation.

If the public school, after evaluating a student, recommends that the child needs a private school because the district cannot meet the child's needs, then the school district must pay the private school tuition. When it is possible, school district personnel will recommend another public school in the area that can provide the necessary services, and the state will bear the cost of transporting the student to that school.

Sometimes parents choose to send their child with a learning disability to a private school. Under the current law, when parents decide on their own that their child would be better off in a private school than in a public one, they cannot submit the tuition bill to the public school district and expect it to be paid. Even so, the student does have a right to receive related services, such as counseling, tutoring, or speech therapy from the school district. Private schools also receive some federal funds for providing special services for students with disabilities. Exactly how much special help private school students are entitled to receive and where that help will be given are complex issues and are interpreted differently in different states. To find out more about the regulations and how they apply in a particular area, you can contact one of the advocacy organizations listed at the end of this book.

As long as a student is attending a public school and his or her parents have approved the IEP, that young person cannot be cut off from receiving help. According to the 1997 amendments to IDEA, an LD student caught using or selling drugs or carrying a weapon to school may be suspended from classes for as long as 45 days, but during that time he or she must continue getting special services.

The school also has a right to change without parental consent, the placement of students who use or sell drugs or carry a weapon to school. For example, an LD student might be pulled from the classroom and required to work with tutors or home-bound teachers during the suspension. If the child is a danger to him or herself or to other students, public school officials can remove students who are covered by IDEA from the classroom for up to 45 days if they get an injunction from a hearing officer.

If an LD student breaks a law, is found guilty, and sentenced to a correctional facility, then the state and the school districts do not have to provide them with the special educational services. The law gives the corrections system the authority to decide how the young person should be educated.

Getting an Equal Chance

Section 504 of the Rehabilitation Act

In the mid 1990s students with learning disabilities who attended Boston University were angry at school president Jon Westling's decision to do away with special programs for students with learning disabilities and to deny students reasonable accommodations. Westling had said publicly that he thought many students who claimed to have learning disabilities were faking the problem. He ordered that all Boston University students who were diagnosed with a learning disability when they entered the school be retested by physicians or psychologists instead of learning specialists. Although he had no training in learning disabilities, he became personally involved with several students' cases and denied them accommodations. He also refused to modify a foreign language requirement that effectively stopped many students with LD from obtaining degrees, and he forbade course substitutions. Since IDEA does not protect the rights of students after graduation from high school, he felt it was his right as president of the university to make the changes.

Several students filed a class action lawsuit against the school on behalf of 480 students with LD who attended BU. In 1997 they won. The court awarded damages to the students who had filed and ordered the university to remove its retesting policy. The university was also ordered to allow the course substitutions because it had not proven that allowing students with LD to take other courses instead of foreign language classes would lower academic standards.

According to U.S. Federal District Court judge Patti Saris, the laws that Westling had violated were section 504 of the Rehabilitation Act of 1973 and the Americans with Disabilities Act (ADA). Both laws forbid any institutions that receive federal money, including schools amd colleges, from discriminating against people with disabilities.

Although the equal access that these laws require was used most often in the past by people with mobility disabilities to force the building of accommodations such as wheelchair ramps and wider doorways, recently it has become a tool to remove barriers that keep students with learning disabilities from having the same access to education as other students do. By discriminating against students because of their learning disabilities, Boston University was found to be violating their civil rights according to the court's decision. The case was a very important one and was closely observed by colleges and universities across the United States.

Section 504 of the Rehabilitation Act prohibits both intentional and unintentional discrimination against people who have disabilities, people who are believed to have disabilities, and their family members. It is different from IDEA in several ways. Parents who sue a school district under IDEA hope to win special programs and services for a student with learning disabilities so that he or she can obtain an education equal to that provided for other students. IDEA, while requiring public schools to offer special help for students with disabilities, provides funding for them to use in order to set up the necessary programs. Specific disabilities are listed as being covered by IDEA. People who have a disability that is not on the list are not covered by the law. The age above which students are no longer covered under IDEA varies from state to state, but it is usually 22.

People with disabilities or their parents who sue educational institutions to obtain their rights under Section 504 are asking for the removal of barriers that prevent disabled students from having the same access to an education as other students have. The Rehabilitation Act does not provide money for schools to remove the barriers to equal access. It does apply to educational agencies that receive federal money for any of their programs, which includes most private schools. The definition of a disability is much broader in Section 504 than in IDEA. Section 504 protects all people who have physical or mental impairment that substantially limits one or more major life activities and who have a record of the impairment or are regarded as having it. The law considers learning a major life activity. Section 504 has no age limit.

Court decisions based on Section 504 have stated that schools are bound to provide reasonable modifications and that the students must be able to meet the degree program's requirements. If Boston University had proven that taking foreign language classes was an essential part of the knowledge that a degree from the school represented, then requiring all students to take one would not necessarily be considered discriminatory.

Like IDEA, Section 504 requires both public elementary and secondary schools to find and identify students with disabilities and to evaluate them. Individual school districts are allowed to decide who will be on the team that decides a student's placement. The placement, like that mandated by IDEA, must be in the least restrictive environment. The districts are not required to let parents be a part of the team under section 504, and although parents are to be notified of their child's evaluation and placement, they do not have to give their consent. Students and parents file Section 504 complaints against the school district with the Office for Civil Rights of the U.S. Department of Education if they feel discrimination has taken place. They can also file against the school district in federal court. So far most schools have not paid much attention to Section 504. Many only evaluate students who fall under the provisions of IDEA. As more parents and college students become aware of the law, it will be used more often.

Americans with Disabilities Act

The Americans with Disabilities Act, which was signed into law in 1990, protects the civil rights of people with disabilities, including learning disabilities. Congress passed it to insure equal opportunity, full participation, independent living, and economic self-sufficiency for these people. The focus of ADA is the workplace. This law prohibits discrimination by employers of 15 or more employees, employment agencies, or labor organizations against qualified individuals. Employers cannot discriminate against workers with a disability in the application process, hiring, advancement, training, wages, or firing. Accommodations that might be required by this law include modifying equipment or restructuring the job so that it still would be done efficiently but could be performed by an employee with a disability, including a learning disability.

ADA also forbids discrimination by state and local governments, departments, and agencies and by companies providing goods, services, and accommodations, such as restaurants, hotels, convention centers, grocery stores, and recreation centers. It applies to all businesses, no matter what the size. In addition, ADA requires the Federal Communications Commission (FCC) to make certain that hearing- and speech-impaired people have access to accommodations as part of their telephone service.

People who believe they have been discriminated against in violation of ADA may bring a civil action in federal court. In addition to awarding money to the person who has brought the suit, the judge can also fine the school, business, or government organization $50,000 for the first violation and $100,000 for subsequent violations. To protect people who assert their rights under ADA the law prohibits employers from coercing employees or retaliating against the person with the disability or anyone trying to help them.

Asking for Help

Even though people with learning disabilities have legal rights, they still may encounter problems. For example, a classroom teacher who hasn't been trained in LD might not understand how to teach material in a way a student diagnosed with a learning disability can understand, or a counselor might tell a student with LD that he or she can't take a class the student wants to try. Waiting for someone else to notice you have a problem and to decide to do something to solve it for you is a sure way to make yourself miserable—whether you have a learning disability or not. It's also a sign of learned helplessness.

For example, not raising your hand to ask a teacher a question or not asking him or her to repeat instructions because people might think you are dumb practically guarantees low grades. Not asking your parents for help on homework that you don't understand because you don't want to bother them may mean that they will be extremely bothered when they see your report card.

The following are some reasons young people with learning disabilities don't ask for help.

- They are trying to hide the fact that they have an LD.
- They think that asking for help is a sign of weakness.
- They don't know how to ask for help.

Waiting until the last possible minute to send out an SOS can spell disaster. People, even well-meaning people, aren't mind readers. They don't know what someone else wants or needs unless told. Keeping quiet about what they need causes young people to resent the fact that nothing seems to go their way. Those resentments can build up into an attitude problem. If a person waits to ask for help until they feel angry or have begun to feel like a failure, when they finally do speak up, the words usually come out all wrong.

In order to get help young people with LD must be honest about their learning disability, both with themselves and with others. Recognizing when to seek a helping hand is a sign of strength, not weakness, and asking for help is not the same as trying to get someone else to do it for you. Sometimes people need to learn to ask for it, and if help is not forthcoming, then they need to stick up for themselves by being persistent. Sometimes a situation requires patience and sometimes it requires fighting for one's legal rights.

Even though Wanda felt like giving up, she kept on trying. Caught between feeling like a dummy at school and being accused of not applying herself at home, she was miserable. Whenever she suggested to her parents that she might need to take special classes, they disagreed. "You aren't making enough effort," her dad accused. "There's nothing wrong with you except laziness." When he threatened to take away her TV privileges, she became furious. "I hardly ever watch television," she yelled at him. "Every night I come home from school and do homework until I go to bed. I can't try any harder than that!"

The next morning her anger pushed her to the school guidance counselor's office where she intended to find out about child abuse laws and see if she could move to a foster home. When the whole story came out and the counselor had looked at Wanda's school records, she asked her parents to come to the school for a conference.

As the day of the meeting approached, Wanda was nervous. No matter how angry she was with her parents and their impossible standards, she didn't want to make trouble for them. Maybe it would have been better if she'd just run away, she thought. At first the meeting didn't go smoothly, but Wanda's counselor persisted in telling her parents the facts about LD and how giving permission for Wanda to be tested and, if necessary, to receive special help could mean the difference between success and failure.

Wanda watched the expression on her father's face when he finally listened to what the counselor was saying. His voice broke, and he almost looked like he might cry when he told about dropping out of school when he was 16 because he couldn't do the work. "I've never talked about this before," he said staring at the floor. "I can barely read, and it's held me back all my life. I want my daughter to do better." Wanda was so shocked, it took awhile for her tears to start. Going against her family to get help from an outsider hadn't been easy, but it had been worth it. Her father's secret had caused too much pain for it to continue.

Her parents gave their permission for the school to give diagnostic tests, and her dad even joked that maybe he should be taking them. The counselor agreed. "LD runs in families," she explained. When she told him about a literacy program at the community college that offered LD testing, he didn't commit to go there, but Wanda noticed he folded the paper about the program the counselor handed him and carefully put in his pocket as if he didn't want to lose it.

Before you can even begin to ask for help, you need to figure out exactly what it is you need. It might be an explanation of how to work problems with fractions or maybe a small electronic spell checker for English class. Perhaps you need help finding out how to deal with someone who is teasing you and just won't stop. Or maybe you need some assistance in figuring out what to do about a teacher who refuses to provide any accommodations in the classroom. Because some forms of learning disabilities make it difficult for people to focus and choose the right words, it is a good idea to write down what it is you are asking for. You might also write down questions you want to ask. That way if you forget what you were going to say in the middle of the conversation, you can have a handy reminder.

Next you need to figure out who can provide the help. Some people might be willing to give assistance but they don't have the knowledge or the resources. For instance, parents can help with homework sometimes, but not if they don't know the answers to the questions you are asking. Parents are not teachers, and your assignments may be over their heads. If someone says, "Sorry, but I can't help," don't give up. Find someone else to ask who might be able to provide the help you need. Having a number of places to turn for help is called having a support network. This network increases the chances that you will find someone who can lend a hand when you need it.

Some people that students with learning disabilities might turn to for help are

- teachers, who can explain assignments and clarify instructions
- parents, who can sometimes help with homework and serve as advocates with the school
- tutors, who can help with academic subjects
- homework hot lines sponsored by schools, which provide assistance on assignments
- friends, who can serve as study partners
- school counselors, who can help work at problem solving and connect students with resources
- school administrators, who can provide accommodations and special services
- learning disabilities advocates connected with groups listed in the back of this book, who can provide information about LD and tips on how to cope with it

One of the most effective ways to get what you want is to pick a good time to ask for it. If the washing machine has just overflowed your baby brother is screaming, and someone is knocking at the door, that is not the time to ask your mother to quiz you on your spelling words! Wait until things have calmed down a bit, or if you need help right now, ask someone else. When your teacher is rushing to finish telling the class homework instructions before the bell rings in 30 seconds, he or she isn't going to stop everything to notice your hand waving in the air. Wait until after the bell rings. The same goes for talking with counselors, school administrators, and learning disabilities advocates. If you walk into their office and demand help immediately, you may not get it. Instead, make an appointment.

How you ask for something often determines whether or not you get it. Think about it. If you were a teacher and a student asked for help, saying, "You never have time for me, and I'm failing English, so tell me what the parts of speech are right now!" how would you respond? If you are like most people, you might feel more than a little irritated and defensive. How would you feel if someone asked you for the same thing, using different words: "I'm feeling overwhelmed by the parts of speech right now. Can you explain the difference between a preposition and an adverb?"

What is the main difference between the two requests for help? The first one blames and demands. The second one simply states the facts without accusing anyone or putting anyone down.

Take a few deep breaths and *calmly* ask for what you want in an assertive manner. Being assertive means you are not too timid and not too bold or angry. You have a right to help from the school system, but you do not have a right to bully people or make them feel guilty in order to get it. Politeness and persistence increase your chances of obtaining a useful response to your request.

6

School Skills: Learning How to Learn

G ary didn't believe he would learn anything in the special classes he attended each morning. He didn't like being singled out. Instead of paying attention to his new teacher, for the first few weeks he tried to block out everything she said. Not until his parents told him they would not buy the skateboard he wanted unless he made an effort, did he start paying attention in class. To his surprise, it wasn't that difficult for him to improve his grades when he followed his teacher's suggestions. He liked using the computers in the new classroom to learn math and reading as well as social studies. The more successes he had, the better he felt about himself and the better he wanted to do.

Soon after Wanda's dyslexia was diagnosed, she began receiving help from a tutor. She liked the individualized instruction, and slowly she began to master many of the skills she hadn't been able to before. One trick her tutor taught her was to trace letters with her finger and then write them while saying the sounds they represented. At first she felt silly when she did it, but before long, words printed on the page began making sense to her. When her reading began to improve, she was amazed to discover that she actually liked to read even though it was still somewhat more difficult for her than for other students.

Although Nathan liked the idea of going into a field that had something to do with sports after he graduated, schoolwork remained low on his list of immediate priorities. "I'll get around to it," he would tell his parents when they asked if he had done his homework. Somehow he never seemed to find the time. There was always a good show on TV or somewhere to go with his friends. When he wasn't doing those things, he practiced songs on an old guitar his uncle had given him.

Teachers and school districts aren't the only ones responsible for how much a student learns. Young people with learning disabilities can increase their success in school by becoming familiar with the unique ways in which they gain knowledge and the problems that make certain kinds of learning difficult for them. They can also use what researchers have discovered about the ways people learn and recall information to improve their ability to remember what they have learned and to develop good study skills, which not only improve grades but make learning easier.

Everyone has his or her own method of learning. Those styles reflect the ways in which we process or perceive information. For example, some people go about learning in a very logical way. They like to find things out one step at a time and feel most comfortable when each piece of information builds on the one before it. They often find it easier to understand material when it contains numbered lists. Orderly, logical learners are the type of people who solve a jigsaw puzzle by starting at one corner or edge and methodically work from there to make the picture appear.

Other people learn in an intuitive way. They read a little here and then a little there, and all of a sudden you hear them say, "Ah hah!" In a sudden flash of insight, they have pulled all those bits and pieces together. The intuitive way to solve a jigsaw puzzle would be to start randomly hooking pieces together. If you looked at an intuitive learner's work, you'd see little clusters of pieces put together all over the table. At the very last minute these clusters fit together to make a recognizable picture.

We learn more easily when the person helping us has a teaching style that matches our individual learning style. Think about your favorite teachers from the past—the ones who made even normally difficult things seem easy to learn. These could be teachers you had in school or out of the classroom, such as a grandmother who taught you to make sugar cookies or a coach who helped you do well in soccer. How well you got along with the person teaching you most likely had an influence on your learning. More important, the way he or she presented the material and the activities was what helped you to catch on.

Discovering Your Learning Style

Before our brains process information, make connections, and find meaning, we have to perceive that information through our senses. Most of us are better at processing information that comes to us from one sense than from the others. To find out your strongest way of perceiving the world around you, read the following questions and answer them on a piece of paper.

1. I get the most information from classes in which the teacher
   a. does a good deal of lecturing and explains what I need to know.
   b. uses the blackboard and overhead projector.
   c. has us do experiments and assigns projects.
2. When I'm reading my textbooks
   a. I find myself reading the hard parts out loud.
   b. the first thing I notice on the page are the maps, diagrams, and graphs.
   c. I get frustrated, so to be honest, I usually don't read them.
3. The way I remember something best is to
   a. hear it several times.
   b. picture it in my mind.
   c. write it down over and over.
4. To relax I like to
   a. listen to music or the radio.
   b. see a good movie.
   c. make something or fix something.
5. If somebody is giving me directions
   a. all they need to do is tell me how to get there.
   b. they need to draw me at map.
   c. once I follow the person, I've got it down.
6. When I'm not sure of the way to spell a word, I
   a. sound it out and go from there.
   b. write it down to see if it looks right.
   c. write the word in the air with my finger.
7. When I'm figuring out a problem in my life, I
   a. think out loud by talking to myself.
   b. make a list.
   c. just jump right in and solve it as I go.
8. People tell me that
   a. they catch me talking to myself.
   b. I have a good sense of color.
   c. I talk with my hands.

If your answers were mostly As, you are what learning researchers call an auditory person; you learn best by hearing things. Mostly Bs for answers means you learn with your eyes. You are a visual person, and for you a picture really is worth a thousand words. If most of your answers were Cs, that indicates you are a tactile, or kinesthetic, person. You do best with a hands-on or learning-by-doing approach. People whose answers are evenly mixed between As, Bs, and Cs feel comfortable learning new things in a number of different ways. The three styles of perception aren't mutually exclusive for most people, but a learning disability can make using one of these styles extremely difficult.

Learning theorist who *have studied sensory processing have found the following:*

Auditory Learners

- remember written material best by saying it out loud.
- catch on more quickly if they hear something.
- do well in classrooms where the teacher lectures.
- easily follow verbal directions.
- don't notice body language very much.

Visual Learners

- have difficulty following spoken directions and lectures.
- pay close attention to body language and like to see people who are speaking.
- make a lot of diagrams and doodles on the notes they make.
- make pictures in their minds.
- do best with written directions and learn well from books.

Tactile/Kinesthetic Learners

- learn by doing.
- also learn by watching someone doing something then imitating them.
- like hand-on projects, workbooks, and field trips.

- enjoy moving their bodies through activities such as running, sports, and dancing.
- often are "huggers"

Thinking about thinking is called *metacognition*. Taking the time to discover how we think and learn is a useful exercise for anyone. When we know what works best for us and find practical ways to apply that information, education becomes easier, both in and out of the classroom.

If you are an auditory learner and have difficulty learning from printed material, some things you might want to try in order to learn more easily are

- using a tape recorder to tape lectures in addition to taking notes;
- reading out loud spelling words, vocabulary words, or anything you need to memorize into your recorder and playing them back until you remember them; and
- sitting at the front of the classroom so that other students don't distract you.

Visual learners can help themselves achieve more in school by trying simple tricks, such as

- color-coding notes and reading assignments with high-lighters (If you aren't allowed to write in your textbook, photocopy it);
- using index cards to make flash cards of the material to be memorized; and
- drawing flowcharts, graphs, maps, and pictures of what is heard or read to help remember.

Kinesthetic learners, who learn best by doing things, might

- repeatedly write words, dates, or other information they need to remember;

- learn math concepts by using and moving around physical objects such as uncooked spaghetti strands or buttons;
- use a calculator for homework assignments; and
- check with teachers to see if they can do a project or experiment for some of their classes instead of writing a paper.

These simple ways of accommodating learning styles are just a start. Once a child, young person, or adult is diagnosed with LD, learning specialists can come up with many more learning techniques that are tailored to individual strengths and weaknesses. The learning specialist also works with a student's classroom teachers so that they can find ways to present material in a manner that makes it easier for a student with LD to understand and remember.

Making Your Memory Work for You

Everyone forgets things that they want to remember sometimes, but people with learning disabilities often have a very hard time recalling information when they need it. Just as not all learning styles are the same, the ways people have of remembering can be different too. Memory problems can happen in just one or in several parts of the memory process. When someone has a hard time recalling information, he or she may have experienced difficulty registering what was going on or holding it in short-term memory, much like trying to catch the words to a song on a radio station with a lot of static. The person might have had a difficult time labeling the information he/she perceived or storing it in long-term memory where it remains until needed. Perhaps the brain couldn't find where it is stored in long-term memory.

Imagine for a moment that you are trying to find a particular car chase scene from a movie on a videotape, but you aren't quite sure when the scene happened. You put the tape in the VCR and fast-forward it to about the place where you think the scene has been recorded. Then you watch the movie for a few seconds. If you've gone too far, you rewind. If you haven't gone far enough, you keep fast-forwarding, stopping and looking for clues about whether the scene has already played or is coming later on the tape. Using this trial and error method might take you quite awhile. Someone with LD goes through a similar, just as frustrating process many times every day.

People with learning disabilities seem to have the most difficulty recalling information they are expected to memorize verbatim, or word for word. This type of remembering is also called *rote memorization.* It includes items you are expected to pull from your memory bank and quickly reproduce exactly as you learned them. Tests that ask you to list or name things also require rote memorization skills. In school you also use rote memorization when you learn

- the multiplication tables
- the bones in the human body
- historical dates
- the names of the states and their capitals
- vocabulary words
- passages from literature or historical documents, such as the Preamble of the United States Constitution

In our daily lives we are often expected to exactly recall

- people's names
- addresses
- telephone numbers
- important dates, such as people's birthdays

Life would be simpler for people with LD if they never had to memorize anything, but knowing the facts is essential in order to do many of the other things expected of us in school, including explaining, analyzing, and comparing—tasks many people with LD are quite good at. In some cases, students with learning disabilities can improve school performance by finding ways to get around having to memorize some pieces of information. Often, a student's IEP will instruct his or her teachers to allow the use of aids that substitute for memorizing. For example, an LD student taking a chemistry class might not be required to learn the table of elements along with the other students. Instead, his or her learning disability might be accommodated by allowing the student to refer to the table when working on assignments or on tests.

Some other memory substitutes are

- looking things up in a dictionary or encyclopedia;
- using a spell checker on a computer to catch spelling mistakes;
- making use of a calculator to do math problems; and
- making use of maps, charts, time lines, and diagrams.

Can you think of any other ways a student with a learning disability could avoid having to memorize something but still be able to use that information?

In some subjects, constantly looking up information is impractical. Languages are a good example of this. Many students with learning disabilities have extreme difficulty learning second languages for this reason. Although you could find every vocabulary word in your French or Spanish dictionary whenever you needed to speak or write them, that process would take too long. Sometimes teachers can modify the way they teach a language in order to help a learning disabled student. Other times the student and teacher may both decide that a student's learning a second language isn't worth the struggle it involves.

The pressure and stress of taking tests can make trying to remember something even more difficult. Add that to a learning disability and the results can be academic disaster.

Gary tries to come across as a tough guy, but when it comes to taking tests, he panics. Even though he acts like he doesn't care if he passes or fails, he can't fool himself. His churning stomach, sweating hands, and pounding heart all tell him that he's scared—frightened that he's about to prove to himself and to the world one more time that he's stupid.

To understand how stress affects learning and memory, remember how you acted and felt when you were searching for something you thought you'd lost such as a T shirt that you had your heart set on wearing that day for school. As you started looking, you knew the school bus would be coming any minute. When you couldn't find the shirt right away, you might have frantically started going through your messy room, your drawers, and then your closet, throwing clothes over your shoulder as you went, your stomach tied in knots. The less time you had to look for it, the more crazy your search might have grown. The angrier and more stressed you became, the crazier your search might become until the horn honking at the end of the driveway meant you threw on any old shirt—and forgot your lunch and your homework—as you ran to catch the bus before it pulled away. Later when you came home from school, you might have seen the shirt neatly folded on the corner of your desk where you'd put it the night before.

When they take tests, sometimes people who have LD frantically rummage through their mental filing cabinets, put down any old answer, and remember the right one as soon as they leave the room. Fortunately it doesn't have to be that way, not when they understand how memory works and learn some simple strategies to help it work more effectively. For example, finding the car chase scene on the videotape we talked about earlier would be much simpler if you noted down the number on the VCR counter when you were watching the movie and the scene occurred. Later on you could have fast-forwarded the tape to the exact spot you wanted. If you always put your T shirts in one place, you could have easily found the one you wanted before the bus arrived.

Tricks that help you better recall information are called *mnemonics*. They are based on what researchers know about the memory process. Before we can remember something we need to perceive it. To do that a person must be able to pay attention and block out distraction. After information is registered, it must be stored. Some people label and store the information that they encounter neatly. Other people's brains seem to have difficulty knowing where to put things. The final part of the memory process is being able to pull the right name or date or spelling from all the information stored in your brain.

Repeat After Me . . . Astounding Memory Tricks

If you try the following memory tricks, chances are one or two will work for you—whether you have a learning disability or not.

1. Only memorize what you absolutely have to. Most of the time you aren't expected to memorize an entire textbook word for word or every single part of the human body. If you're not sure what facts, figures, names, and dates need to be memorized by rote for a test, ask the teacher.

2. Compare what you are trying to remember to something else. This connection is called an *analogy*. Ask yourself what this new fact or word or date reminds you of. Maybe to you, the American Civil War seems like football, which happens to be your favorite sport. When you think of it that way and imagine the generals as being team members for the Union and the Confederacy, you have an easier time remembering their names.

3. Organize the material you are learning by putting it into categories or finding patterns in it. For instance, if you are working on memorizing the bones in the human body, your job will be easier if you group the informa-

tion together, studying all of the hand bones together, then all of the foot bones, and so on. Sometimes it helps to make a chart when you categorize things. If you are trying to remember who won the major battles of the Civil War, draw a line down the center of a sheet of paper and make two lists, one for battles won by the North and one for those won by the South.

4. If what you are trying to memorize doesn't seem to have a pattern, then invent one. Acronyms are a handy way of doing this if you need to recall several things. When you make an acronym, you take the first letter of each thing you will need to remember and make a word out of those letters. Many people learn the colors of the rainbow and the order in which they appear by memorizing the name Roy G. Biv, which stands for red, orange, yellow, green, blue, indigo, and violet.

5. You can also try using the first letter of every word in a sentence to remember something. For instance, "Every good boy deserves fudge," stands for all the notes on lines of music.

6. Yet another way to make a pattern for information you are learning, especially lists of things you need to remember in order, is to make up a story that hooks them together. The sillier the story you make up, the higher the chances are that you will remember it. Just be sure that it makes sense and hangs together.

7. Make your learning style works for you. If you are an auditory learner, speak whatever it is you are memorizing. Sometimes it helps to read the textbook aloud. Auditory learners can also help themselves remember things by making rhymes out of what they need to know; for example, "In 1492 Columbus sailed the ocean blue," or "*i* before *e* except after *c*." Another trick for auditory learners is to chant the material they need to remember.

Visual learners can make their memory work better by picturing images of the material in their minds. For example, a person could picture a fishing pier in the middle of South Dakota to remember that Pierre is that state's capital. Usually the sillier the mental picture you can come up with, the easier it will be to remember the name of the fact. Homemade flash cards made from index cards can boost a visual learners' memory power. Drawing graphics, charts, and maps works as well.

Kinesthetic learners tend to remember things better if they pace back and forth or keep time on the table with their hand as they chant the material they need to know. A kinesthetic learner trying to remember the formula for finding the perimeter of something would probably have an easier time if he or she experimented with a piece of string and a ruler to feel how the formula actually worked. Learning the bones of the human body would be easier if the student actually touched the part of their body to feel the bone beneath the skin as he or she said the name of it.

8. Rehearse what you've learned. Practice makes perfect. Imagine what it would be like to star in a play and be asked to walk out onto the stage in front of an audience after only having time to read through your lines one time. Probably you wouldn't make it past the first act. Like acting, test performance depends on practicing—recalling the information over and over again until you are confident that you know where it is stored and how to get it. One way to rehearse is to have someone quiz you about what you've read or were supposed to memorize. On your own, you might want to practice writing the information, whether it is dates, names of the parts of speech, or your spelling words. Rehearsal works best if you make it a part of your studying, asking yourself questions and practicing recall after learning small pieces of information instead of trying to memorize everything right before the test. You can practice things you have to memorize while you are waiting for the bus, doing dishes, or in the shower.

Take some time to check out how these memory tricks work. Imagine you need to remember the words *kite, puppy, Declaration of Independence, popcorn,* and *flower* in order to be able to repeat them in order on a test. Try making a story out of these five things. Once upon a time . . . As you tell yourself the story, see it happening in your mind. Tell yourself the story out loud three times. Now close this book and write down the five things you had to memorize. How well were you able to remember?

Study Skills for School Success

When Nathan tried to settle down and give his schoolwork his best shot like his parents and teachers advised, he had a terrible time. In the first place, he didn't know where to begin. Everybody acted as if he should have been born knowing how to study, but he didn't have a clue. To keep them happy, he'd sit at the desk in his room with an open book in front of him for an hour or so at night, but his mind would wander everywhere except to the schoolwork in front of him. Studying doesn't have to be a form of torture, not if you know how to do it right. In fact, the better you are at using good study skills, the less time you will need to spend doing schoolwork.

Smart study habits begin in the classroom and like the other strategies discussed in this chapter, they work for students without learning disabilities as well as for those who have them. Some of them are deceptively simple. For example, where a student sits in the classroom can have a big impact on learning. When you sit at the front of the room, not only is it easier to hear and see what is going on, there's much less chance of being distracted by what other students are doing. Asking questions when you don't understand the material is another simple tactic that works wonders, as does listening to what the teacher is saying.

Taking notes is not only a method to help remember what is being said, it is also a way to focus your attention. Learn to listen for the main points and write them down. Trying to get every word the teacher says on paper is a lost cause. If you use a tape recorder to record classes, use it to teach yourself to be a good note taker. Even though the recorder is on, write down notes. After class listen to the tape and rewrite your notes highlighting the main points. (Make sure to label your tapes so you can find them later.)

Having a special place for studying at home is a good idea too. Be sure that your study space has good lighting and gives you enough area to spread out your textbook, notebooks, and other materials. Having a place where you regularly study helps to get you in the mood to learn. It doesn't need to be fancy to work.

Wanda's parents couldn't afford a desk or her own private office, but she did have a room of her own, and her mom gave her a card table. Wanda found some sturdy boxes she could cover with material. Her dad donated some file folders that were being discarded from his work, and Wanda found some inexpensive baskets at the thrift store she could use to keep pens, paper clips, and rubber bands in order. Making her study corner was fun, and when it was finished, she actually found herself looking forward to using it.

The best study spaces have few distractions. You know what bothers you when you are trying to concentrate. Is it people talking? The noise from the television set? Someone walking past in your field of vision? What above clutter? Many people learn more effectively when they are listening to music without words. The same people may be distracted by listening to songs with lyrics. They start out focusing on the material in front of them, but before they know it, they are listening to the words of the song. Begin noticing the things that distract you when you are trying to study and make an effort to eliminate them from your study environment.

Once you have a practical place to study, you need to figure out what to do while you are there. Telling yourself that you are going to be serious about studying and that you intend to remember helps to focus your mind on the task at hand. Even though this trick may sound simple, it works. Many of us have absolutely no problem remembering all the movies our favorite actor played in or the batting averages of dozens of major league baseball players, but we can't remember the name of the vice president or a science formula.

If your mind starts to wander as you study, remind yourself to pay attention to what you are doing. You may find it helpful to think of a way to reward yourself for studying by treating yourself to something you want afterward. For example, you may decide that after doing schoolwork for an hour, you will take a break to watch a short TV program. When it's done, discipline yourself to get back to your studies.

As you do your assignments, make sure you understand what you are trying to learn. If the material doesn't mean anything to you, then you probably won't be able to remember it no matter how hard you try. First try hooking new information to something you already know and understand well or try to put it in a bigger context. For example, if you are studying the history of the Revolutionary War and need to remember all about the Battle of Lexington, ask yourself what came before it and afterward. Sometimes learning vocabulary words is easier if you find out what the parts of the words mean. Often those parts are Greek or Latin. Knowing that *geo* means earth and *ology* means the study of something, makes it easier to figure out the meaning of the word *geology*. If you have a difficult time understanding material, ask your parents, your teacher, another student, or a tutor for help.

Break what you are learning into small pieces. If you're not used to studying or have a difficult time sitting still, begin by studying for 10- or 15-minute blocks. Instead of trying to learn all about the whole Civil War in one night, read and memorize a little bit at a time. Rather than trying to memorize your entire list of spelling words at one sitting, take them five at a time. Allow yourself short breaks in between to get up and walk around.

Learning experts call these mini-study sessions *chunking.* Chunking is based on the fact that the human brain generally can hold only about seven bits of information in short-term memory at the same time before it either stores it in long-term memory or discards it. Breaking a big topic into small pieces during a cramming session the night before a test is almost impossible. Learning material a piece at a time requires time and planning, but it can reduce stress. When you are anxious, your brain is too busy figuring out how you are going to survive to be able to learn new information. Stress also causes us to forget what we have memorized. Try to approach assignments, even difficult ones, calmly so that you will be able to think as clearly as possible and do your best.

Some students with LD suffer from test *anxiety,* which is similar to the stage fright that many actors and actresses experience before they perform. No matter how much they have studied their lines, they are afraid they will forget them once the curtain is raised or the camera starts rolling. No matter how much they have studied, once the test is on the desk in front of students with test anxiety, they are scared that they'll fail. For people with learning disabilities, fear can make remembering impossible. If you have test anxiety, practicing good study skills; getting enough rest the night before the test and making sure you've eaten breakfast can help. Take a few deep breaths and calm down before you begin the test. If your test anxiety is so severe that you can't cope with it on your own, talk to a teacher or counselor for help in managing test stress.

7

Learning to Live with LD

The building seemed more like a maze than a school for Nathan during the first week of high school. He had five different classrooms to find, and on the first day his teachers assigned seats for the classes, so not only did he have to find the classrooms, once he got there he had to find the right seat. Then he had to remember five different teachers' names. He had to remember where his locker was and the combination for it. He had a locker in gym class too, and that one had yet another baffling combination lock.

He was so down on school and on himself for the difficulties he was having that he wouldn't talk to anybody. Finally his dad noticed his attitude change and suggested making a map of the school and labeling it with the names of the classes he was taking and the names of his teachers. He could put it inside of his notebook. He could also write down his locker combinations and carry it on a slip of paper in his pocket. "Then you'll only have to remember two things, instead of twelve" his dad said, "your notebook and the slip of paper." Nathan doubted something so easy would work, but he tried it and to his surprise it did.

As you learned in Chapter Three, LD can affect many areas of life not directly related to academics. These range from finding one's way home from the shopping mall and learning to get along with people to being able to remember where you put your wallet and remembering your best friend's birthday. Very often something as simple as Nathan's map can make a world of difference to people with learning disabilities. When they learn to try "smarter" instead of harder, people with LD can compensate for the tricks their brain seems to play on them. These "try-smarter" strategies, not only help improve how well cope at school and at home, but they make us feel better about ourselves.

Learning disabilities aren't an excuse for not getting along with people or for having a perpetually messy room, and they aren't an excuse for not trying, but they are a major reason why a person with LD might have difficulties getting along, being neat, or trying new things. Pretending that they are not there because we're afraid the people we care about will think we aren't smart, first of all, only makes life harder for us. Often when we try to hide LD, people may think we're being inattentive. They may label us as lazy or rude, when we really aren't. In the second place, it takes a great deal of energy to pretend we don't have LD—energy that could be better used finding creative ways to live with the disability so that it doesn't interfere with our lives.

Wanda felt embarrassed about her dyslexia. Even after the school had diagnosed her and her IEP was in place, she still didn't like to talk about the things that gave her difficulty. Outside of school she wanted to be exactly like everybody else, so, unlike Nathan, she didn't tell her parents the trouble she had following directions that involved right and left or reading the shopping list her mom made for her when she sent her to the store alone. Because Wanda's parents didn't have dyslexia, they weren't aware of the problems she had outside of the classroom. Neither were her friends. Wanda was always self-conscious and felt she had to be perfect so that people wouldn't find out about her LD and maybe feel sorry for her. The fear of being found out made her nervous.

Keeping a secret, especially about something such as LD, causes stress. Much of the stress that people who have learning disabilities experience comes from fear—fear of being discovered just as Wanda felt. Wanda's anxiety causes her to keep to herself more than she would like to. Nathan's fear of having people think he is a scatterbrain sometimes stops him from trying new things. Gary hates surprises. In order to feel okay, he wants to be able to predict what is going to happen next.

Stress and the fears that trigger it, often cause people to be even more disorganized and forgetful than their LD alone would make them. It also causes them to lead unnecessarily limited lives. People with learning disabilities usually have very creative minds. Instead of being ashamed of themselves, they need to learn to use their creativity to find ways of doing things that work for them. Even if their method of getting something done isn't the same as some-one else's, that's perfectly fine.

When people with learning disabilities haven't thought about how LD affects their life or have yet to discover ways of coping, their life seems out of control. Gary's room looks like a hurricane hit it. He can never find anything he needs. Wanda tries to take notes during her classes, but she can't read her own handwriting. Neither can anyone else. Nathan never seems to be able to do anything on time. He feels like he's running around in circles and never catches up. Because he tries to do everything at once, often he ends up getting nothing done at all.

Goal Setting: Putting First Things First

One way out of the LD confusion is to figure out what things you really need and want to do. Then invest your energy and your time on those and don't sweat the small stuff. No one, whether he/she has a learning disability or not, can do everything. Before you read further, take some time to sit back, close your eyes, and imagine you are an old person, even older than your grandparents are today. As an elderly man or woman looking back on all the years of your life, what do you think you would consider as having been the most important things you'd done? Probably these would be the things that made you the happiest and that you felt the proudest of doing.

Think about how you spend your days now. How much are you doing that is important to you or that will help you to eventually get where you want to be in the future? If you're like most people, you spend many hours doing things you don't need to do, such as watching TV, listening to music, or hanging out with friends. You may also spend time doing things you neither need nor want to do—wasting time.

Wasting time by procrastinating, putting off activities, is one of the biggest booby traps for people with LD.

Gary delays doing homework until it is too late to do the work. He sits in front of the TV watching shows he's not interested in for hours on end. As a result his grades are lower than they would have been had he at least turned in some of his work. He's been procrastinating so long that he doesn't know how to break the habit. The longer he puts off doing something, the less he wants to do it and so he stalls further. The higher the work piles up, the harder it seems to him. Procrastination is no fun. The more Gary drags his feet, the worse he feels about himself and the more he worries about never being able to catch up.

People procrastinate for many reasons. Gary puts off taking care of his schoolwork because it is an unpleasant job and because he is afraid that he will fail. Wanda delays doing many of the things she's expected to do both at school and at home because she's certain she can't do anything right. "Why bother?" is her attitude. Nathan doesn't worry about failing, and he doesn't dislike work. He simply forgets what it was he was supposed to do, or he'll start to do one thing and get sidetracked by another.

Some people with learning disabilities feel overwhelmed with all the things they need to do and they have no idea how to start. Others, because of their LD symptoms, have difficulty keeping track of time. They struggle with both telling time and sensing how much time has gone by. Other reasons why a person might procrastinate are

- they spend so much time planning something, they never have time to start it.
- their standards are too high; because they want to do everything perfectly, they spend too much time on details and don't know when to quit and move on to something else.
- they are angry but afraid to tell anyone directly, so they go on "strike."
- boredom has them stuck in a rut.
- they like the excitement that doing things at the last possible minute gives them.

Even though the reasons for wasting time by procrastinating are many, the solution is a simple one: planning by setting goals based on what is important and then breaking them into small pieces and setting deadlines. Instead of ovewhelming yourself, you can achieve what you need to do one small step at a time—and in the process, conquer procrastination.

Some Timely Hints

Before you can start to plan your time, you need to take a close look at how you spend it. Try this experiment. Pretend you are a scientist studying how long it takes you to do things. For two or three days carry a small notebook and a watch with you. Instead of guessing how long it takes you to shower and dress in the morning, eat breakfast, or do your homework, time yourself and write down the facts. See if you can account for every minute of your day including the times you are watching television, listening to the radio, or just hanging out. You might be surprised at how you spend your time.

Keeping a record of your time can help you in two ways. The first thing you can learn from a daily journal is how long it takes you to do activities. It might feel like doing the dishes takes about an hour, when really it only takes 15 minutes. Time might fly when you're watching your favorite TV show, and the next one, and just one more after those. Before you know it the entire evening is gone. Keeping a log also helps you to find your time wasters so you can do something about them.

Time doesn't have to be a foe for people with LD. A few procrastination busters that have helped many people with learning disabilities put time on their side are listed below.

- **set priorities.** Some things are more important to do than others. Number the items in the order of their importance so you can do first things first.
- **keep your goals reasonable.** Don't bite off more than you can chew or mentally beat yourself up if you can't finish doing every single thing on your list. The key to

surviving life with a learning disability is to make life as simple as possible.

- **learn to say no.** You cannot possibly do everything everyone in your life would like you to do all the time. You're only human.
- **figure out what you do to waste time,** perhaps talking too long on the phone or watching TV or playing video games. Turn those things into rewards for finishing your work. It is important to remember that not everything that is fun is a waste of time. Everyone needs time to relax. Watching a favorite show is not a time waster—not if you limit the amount of time you spend on these activities and make sure you have the time to get the things you need done.
- **set a routine for the things you must do every day.** Establish specific times when you will do your homework, clean your room, and do chores around the house. Some people with ADD find it helps to write down everything they must do on the schedule, such as brushing their teeth, showering, and eating breakfast. As much as possible, try to stick to your schedule.
- **use a watch** with an alarm or set your alarm clock if you have difficulty keeping track of time. Some people set the alarm a few minutes earlier than they really need to wake up or leave the house in order to be somewhere. That way they are certain they will be on time.
- **make a "to do" list.** Before you go to bed at night make a list of the things you need to do the next day. Then as you accomplish those tasks cross them off your list. You might want to keep a short-term daily list and a longer list of things to do by the end of the week or the end of the month.
- **tackle the hardest things first instead of the easiest.** You'll have more energy to do them, and once they are out of the way, you'll feel better.
- **break the big jobs into parts.** A major assignment, such as writing a paper, has many steps. You must pick a topic,

do your research, take notes, write the rough draft, and then the final one. Set deadlines for yourself for each part of the assignment. By the same token, doing your night's homework is easier if you list all the pieces you need to finish, such as do math problems, read history, and outline oral book report. Small steps are easier to handle than one big overwhelming chunk of work.

- **write down important dates,** such as big tests and friends' birthdays, on a calendar of your very own, so you won't have to use all your energy to remember them.
- **write yourself notes to remind yourself** of especially important things that you need to remember to do. (Post-its are great for this. Stick them in places where you are sure to see them.)
- **be flexible.** Allow some room in your life for surprises. Without surprises life would be very dull.

A final word of advice: If you can't walk and chew gum at the same time, don't try to. Some people with learning disabilities thrive on doing a number of projects at once and move back and forth between them. Each project serves as a break from the others. Not everyone is like that. Find out what style works best for you. Whether you have a 1-track or a 16-track mind, teach yourself to pay attention to what you are doing. Remember, too, that rehearsal isn't limited only to school subjects. If you aren't sure you can find a place you need to be at, take a trial run and go there the day before just to check it out.

When you've taken the time to plan ahead, you don't have to worry about something else you should be doing or fretting over something that already happened and that you couldn't change if your life depended on it. The Buddhists call this living-in-the-moment approach to life *mindfulness*. When you practice it, you are free to rise to the challenge and fully enjoy what you are doing.

A Place for Everything and Everything in Its Place

Time isn't the only thing that people with LD have difficulty organizing. Gary loses jackets, his school books, and once he even his lost his expensive new basketball sneakers. His mother was so mad she didn't talk to him for a week. When Nathan rummages through the desk drawers to look for paper, he pulls out a half-eaten sandwich, his dad's old army medals, the family dog's collar, and two pairs of clean socks, but there's no notebook paper. Since he didn't know he was running out, he didn't tell his mother to get more.

Many people with LD attract stacks of books, papers, CDs, and dirty socks as if they were magnets. The same mental processing problem that causes people to have a hard time organizing their notes or paying attention to one word at a time can cause major hassles in generally keeping their lives organized. To avoid Nathan's plight and make life easier on themselves, people with learning disabilities need to avoid clutter. The fewer visual distractions that get in the way the better. When things that you don't use and may not even want pile up, the mere idea of cleaning up the mess is overwhelming. It's hard to know where to begin. As with everything else, start small. Clean up one small area of your room—or your school locker—at a time. You might want to divide it into quarters or another way that makes sense for you. Going through your closet should be a job in and of itself.

Instead of shoving everything into that closet, which is probably full anyway, or under the bed, or straightening up all those piles of possessions, get two big boxes and label them. One box should be for things you aren't using right now but will need later, such as your winter coat in the middle of summer. The items you will put in the second box are things you no longer use at all. You don't necessarily have to get rid of these things if you're not ready to, but perhaps you can find a place to store them for now. The first box can go in a closet. Find a place for the second one that is out of the way, perhaps in the attic or basement.

Now you need to figure out what to do with the things you use often. Since you can't very well pick things up if you don't know where to put them, decide on places for everything. You might designate a drawer just for school supplies and one for underwear and socks. Instead of cramming everything that will fit beneath your bed, see if you can get some plastic storage boxes or cut down cardboard boxes so they will slide beneath the bedframe and use them as drawers. Label your drawers and storage boxes so that you know what's in them. Get a laundry basket or clothes hamper for your room and toss your dirty clothes into that.

Once you've straightened up, take a few minutes every evening to tidy your room. This would be a good thing to put on your list. By coping with the clutter as it happens, it doesn't pile up and overwhelm you. Besides, 15 minutes a day of tidying up isn't as much torment as, for example, finding out that all your socks are dirty in the morning right before you have to go to school or spending all day Saturday cleaning your room. (To avoid the sock disaster, lay your school clothes out the night before.)

Getting Along with Others

Gary's friends say he has "foot-in-mouth" disease because he speaks the first words that pop into his mind. Sometimes what he says are insults, and people get mad at him. Nathan feels limited in his social life because he can't focus in groups. The one party he went to stressed him out; there were just too many people talking all at once. He tried to have fun, but he couldn't stand it. Wanda has difficulty talking to friends on the phone because if she can't see their expressions, she can't be sure of what they are saying.

Problems like these don't force people with LD to live like hermits or go through life having people believe they are stuck up or mean. Although getting along with friends and family members may sometimes be difficult, there are ways to cope.

Besides respect and kindness, relationships—whether they be with friends, parents, or brothers and sisters—are based on good communication. Even though communication is a big word, its meaning is a simple one: listening and talking. Many things can get in the way when we listen and talk. For instance, if we're angry at someone, we might not pay attention to their side of the story, or we hear it all wrong. If we're worried about a big test tomorrow, we probably aren't going to pay close attention to our friend's description of how her date went last night—even if she is our *best* friend.

The perception and information processing problems of learning disabilities makes listening to what another person is saying and really understanding it more difficult. People who have ADD sometimes don't know what they are feeling because they have a hard time paying attention to their feelings long enough to put a name to them. Language problems can make it difficult to come up with the right word, even when we know in pictures what it is we want to say.

The listening and talking skills listed below help people with learning disabilities, and those without them, have the kind of conversations that lead to better relationships. Like everything else, we learn them best if we pick one at a time to work on and if we practice, practice, practice!

I Hear You

People can learn to be better listeners if they

- practice paying attention to what the other person is saying instead of letting their minds race ahead to plan what they are going to say. When we think about other things, we wind up hearing the sounds rather than listening to the words or the meaning of what the other person is saying.

- show interest in what the other person has to say by
  - using eye contact
  - not interrupting
  - making encouraging comments, not negative ones
  - trying, for a few minutes at least, to see the world from his or her point of view.
- ask questions when they don't understand what people are saying or how they feel. (Another way of doing this is to rephrase what they have said. For example, "I want to make sure I understand you. You and Charlie broke up.")
- pay attention to more than words. Up to 90 percent of the listening we do is with our eyes. The amount of energy a person has, their gestures, and facial expressions can add meanings to their words.
- find out what the other person might be feeling by asking them or making a comment like, "You seem angry."
- ask questions that require more than a yes or no answer to keep the conversation going.

Getting your point across doesn't have to be difficult. Once you start using the listening skills listed above, talking to people will automatically become easier. If the conversation is an important one, such as discussing your grade with a teacher or trying to resolve a conflict with a family member or friends, take time beforehand to organize your thoughts. Sometimes it helps to make a list of your main points so that you don't forget just what it is you want to communicate. That way you won't get too far off the topic, either, something many people with learning disabilities tend to do.

You increase your chances of having people listen to what you have to say if you are polite when you speak to them. One way to be courteous is to avoid negativity or bossiness. You know you are bossing people around if you hear yourself using words like *never, always, should,* and *ought.* Bossy people often blame others when something goes wrong. They say things such as, "It's all your fault," or "See what you made me do." No one wants to hear that. Remember, as well, to apologize if you make a mistake. Everybody makes mistakes sometimes. No one will think poorly of you if you admit that you aren't perfect; on the contrary, other people get angry at people who insist that they are always right.

Because people with LD don't always pay attention to natural breaks in conversation, sometimes they jump in too fast and cut people off. If people tell you that you are interrupting, practice your listening skills some more or listen to other people's conversations and play detective. See if you can find the clues in conversations that signal the speaker is finished with what he or she has to say. If you have difficulty with this, ask a parent or a good friend to help you practice your conversation skills.

Because they can't see the person they are speaking with, talking on the telephone can be difficult for people who have auditory processing disorders. Many people with LD become confused or forgetful during phone conversations. Some simple telephone techniques can help. Remember to tell the person you called who you are, instead of jumping right into a conversation. If the call is an important one, make a few notes about what you want to say and take notes about what the other person is saying. To avoid distractions, talk on the phone when there isn't a lot of activity in the same room. If the distraction isn't something you can turn off such as a television set or radio, tell the person you will call back at a better time.

Relating and communicating in a room full of people is a challenge for many people with learning disabilities, as well. Even if groups bother you, you don't need to avoid them altogether. Instead practice being in small groups of three of four people for short periods of time to get over your discomfort. As with telephone calls, practice ahead of time with a parent or a close friend you trust. You can plan some of the things you might be able to talk about with other people and practice some conversation-starter questions. Sometimes people with LD feel more confident when they bring a friend to situations that have a high potential for stress. Once you're there, pay attention to how you feel. If you start getting overwhelmed by all that is going on, it's perfectly okay to take a break. Step outside for a while or even take a walk around the block to collect your scattered thoughts. When in doubt, remember your listening skills. People like to be around people who listen to what they have to say.

Resolving Conflicts

It can happen to the best of us. We practice our listening skills and are at our most polite, but still we get into arguments. We disagree with parents about how late we should be allowed to stay out at night. We fight with our brothers or sisters when they borrow something that belongs to us and don't return it or bring it back broken. We get mad at friends when they tease us about something we feel sensitive about. Disagreements, it seems, are just a part of life.

Even though we can't avoid them, we do have choices about how we handle them. We can either impulsively act on our angry feelings by calling people names, saying the first mean thing that comes to mind, or even lashing out with our fists. Or we can step back, take a deep breath and try to talk our differences through in order to get what we want. Which way do you think gives you the highest chances of settling differences and resolving conflicts?

Some young people cope with conflicts by trying to ignore them. Wanda is like that.

When Wanda's parents told her she couldn't take driver's education with the rest of her friends because of her dyslexia and that they would not allow her to actually get behind the wheel, she was very upset. "You don't know your right from your left," her dad told her. "Even if you don't get in an accident, you'll get lost." Although she didn't believe her learning disability would make her an unsafe driver, she didn't say anything. Instead, she hid her angry feelings deep inside. Later they came out in dozens of little ways. She pouted around the house and stopped doing her chores. She picked fights with her younger brother and sister. How do you think Wanda could have gone about solving her problem in a more constructive way?

People with learning disabilities often need time to get a handle on their anger and to decide carefully what they really need to say instead of speaking the first thoughts that pop into their minds. Without taking that time out, they can make the conflict much worse than it started out to be. For instance, a teenager whose parents forbid driving might impulsively take the car for a joyride without asking. The result of that would be that, even though they would get their way for a few hours, they would destroy their chances of gaining their parents' permission to drive for a long time. They would probably be punished for such serious disobedience as well.

One way Wanda, for example, could start to resolve the conflict she has with her parents is to sit down and talk with them. First she could find something about driving they all agree on, such as the fact that she doesn't want to get into a car wreck and either hurt herself or wreck the family automobile. Even though she believes her mom and dad are being overprotective, their concern for her safety is common ground that Wanda can use as a starting point for their discussion.

She could also practice the same assertiveness skills she has learned to use when she asks a teacher for help—speaking up for herself at a time when her parents are more likely to listen and being careful to ask for what it is she wants without accusing or blaming them. "I appreciate your concern for my safety, but I really want to see if I can in learn to drive," she could say when they were in good moods and there were few distractions. She could share her feelings with them, taking responsibility for them by saying, "I feel hurt when you don't have confidence in me," instead of, "You make me feel bad because you don't trust me."

Wanda could look for a compromise, a way to solve the conflict that would give both her and her parents something they want. Some people call this a win-win situation. In order to arrive at win-win situations, people need to fight fair by sticking to the issues at hand. Even though Wanda's anger has her thinking about all the times her parents stopped her from doing things in the past, she needs to focus on the present conflict and come up with a solution for it. She might suggest that they allow her to take the driver's education class and find out what the teacher thinks about the impact of her dyslexia on driving, then take that information into consideration when they make their decision.

Teasing is a form of conflict that all children, young people, and adults with learning disabilities face at some time during their lives. Even when you understand that the person doing the teasing probably doesn't feel very good about him- or herself and is picking on you in a misguided attempt to feel superior, being teased can still cause you to feel terrible. Your first impulse might be to tease back. If someone calls you stupid, then you say they are fat or ugly. Fighting fire with fire only makes the teasing get worse. The teasing that might have begun with an offhand remark can quickly escalate into all-out warfare.

If the teasing is mild, try to give the person doing it the benefit of the doubt. Sometimes people who say cruel things don't understand how deeply they have hurt your feelings. They may think they are only being funny, even if it is at your expense. Perhaps they don't know anything about learning disabilities and are thus revealing their ignorance. It is up to you to make them aware of how you feel and request what you want in a calm and firm way. Keep it short and to the point. You might say something like: "When you call me a dummy, I feel hurt and angry. Please stop doing that. I'm not a dummy, I have a learning disability."

If that doesn't work, try to avoid them. Avoiding someone isn't the same thing as running away from them, it simply means not putting yourself in their vicinity when you don't have to be. Should the teasing get worse, you might need to enlist the help of a teacher or other trusted adult to help you by moving your seat or locker assignment and perhaps talking to the person doing the teasing. In most cases, these strategies will work. In the meantime, work on not letting it bother you. If you feel good about yourself, it is very difficult for other people to bring you down. Besides, you have better things to do with your life than worry about the opinions of others.

8

Rising to the LD Challenge

Albert Einstein nearly failed math when he was in school. According to his own reports, he had what learning specialists would call dyslexia. In spite of his LD, he created the theory of relativity, one of the most far-reaching scientific discoveries of our time.

Thomas Edison's teachers believed he was slow and incapable of learning anything. He stopped his formal education when he was in elementary school, but later went on to take out patents on 1,093 inventions. Among his contributions to our world were the electric lightbulb, the phonograph, and an early kind of movie projector called the tachistoscope.

Robert Louis Stevenson, author of the classic *Treasure Island,* had dyslexia. He got the idea for his frightening book *Dr. Jekyll and Mr. Hyde,* yet another classic, from a dream and said that half of his work was done in his sleep.

Because of his learning disability, Walt Disney could not write well. He began drawing pictures to communicate with people and as a way to express himself. The resulting cartoon characters, including Mickey Mouse and Donald Duck, remain favorites of children today. By making movies using his cartoon characters and building the theme parks Disneyland and Walt Disney World, Disney turned his ideas into a multimillion dollar business empire.

People with learning disabilities are anything but losers. They are not condemned to lead limited lives or to achieve less than other people. In fact, many people with learning disabilities are superachievers. Some other people with LD who have made big contributions to the world are

- Bruce Jenner, Olympic decathlon champion, who turned to sports to raise his self-esteem after learning he had dyslexia
- Tom Cruise, film actor, who is dyslexic and who must learn his lines by having someone read them to him
- Hans Christian Andersen, creator of fairy tales loved by children throughout the world, who had both dyslexia and attention deficit disorder
- Stevie Wonder, popular music composer and performer, who overcame both blindness and a sensory processing problem
- Steven Spielberg, director of the *Star Wars* trilogy, *E.T.,* and many other movies that have entertained millions, who has dyslexia
- British prime minister Winston Churchill, who was dyslexic

All of these people have made positive contributions to the world. Instead of being defeated by their learning disabilities, they used them to improve their own lives and the lives of others. Although their learning disabilities were not easy to live with, these challenges turned out to be gifts, rather than handicaps.

LD: A Blessing in Disguise?

Before you read further, test yourself on how much you know about learning disabilities. Look at the following list of words, which describe the characteristics of a certain kind of person. As you read them, ask yourself what kind of a person you think they describe?

- attracted to and accepting of disorder
- adventurous
- always baffled by something
- defies conventions of courtesies
- discontented
- disturbs organization
- emotionally sensitive
- energetic
- feels the whole parade is out of step with him/herself
- independent thinker
- intuitive
- becomes preoccupied with a problem (hyperfocuses)
- not interested in small details
- stubborn
- temperamental
- somewhat uncultured, primitive
- versatile

These traits all seem to belong to someone with a learning disability, right? Maybe someone with attention deficit hyperactivity disorder or perhaps a language processing disorder such as dyslexia. Although they very well could describe a person with LD, they come from a much longer list that describes instead a person who is creatively gifted. When psychologist E. Paul Torrance compiled the list, the famous psychologist wasn't researching people with learning disabilities. He was studying people he termed *creatively gifted*—people who excel in the arts and in invention. Many of the characteristics on his list are present in a number of people who have learning disabilities—too many to be a coincidence.

Researchers who have studied the creative process in an attempt to find out what it means to think in this way have found that creative geniuses

challenge assumptions. They dare to question things that most people accept as truth on face value alone. They also are willing to trust their hunches more than conventional logic.

see in new ways. To creative thinkers, strange things may seem familiar, and familiar things often seem strange. They also tend to think in images, as did Leonardo da Vinci, who in addition to his paintings worked on a design for a flying machine hundreds of years before the Wright brothers invented the airplane.

recognize patterns. Instead of getting caught up in details, they look at the big picture, seeing major similarities or differences in ideas or events.

make connections. If an original thinker can't find a pattern, he or she is not afraid to combine seemingly unrelated ideas, object, or events in ways that lead to new ideas.

hold opposites together in their minds. Innovative thinkers suspend the normal thinking processes. A conventional thinker will say that something can't be bad and good at the same time, but a creative thinker will say that yes, indeed, that can be so and devise a philosophy to back it up.

take chances. Extremely creative people, whether they are inventors, musicians, or business people, are not afraid of risks. They try new things and are not afraid of other people's opinions.

Conventional thinkers often must take classes or workshops where they are taught the techniques of creativity to help them in their jobs. Many people with learning disabilities are already original thinkers because they were born with brains that seem effortlessly inventive. Even though they have very creative minds, people with LD don't always use this gift. That's because they either don't know how recognize it or they see it as something bad—something that gets in the way of being like everybody else. Often they have been taught that their way of looking at the world is wrong.

Some of the problems creatively gifted people with LD encounter during their school years have more to do with the education system than with their own brains. Schools are designed to educate a large number of people so that they will understand and be able to use basic skills like adding numbers, knowing whether Massachusetts is on the East or West Coast, and reading a newspaper. Although many teachers try to encourage students to think independently and pursue their own interests, that can be very difficult in a classroom containing 25 to 30 pupils. Too often students who require extra attention, who disrupt the teacher's lesson plans, or who don't conform in other ways are seen as nuisances and troublemakers rather than future artists, entrepreneurs, or inventors. Square pegs in round holes, they don't fit into many classrooms because the school system wasn't designed for people like them.

Some of the things that students with learning disabilities are criticized for, and even punished for, aren't really negative. For example, many people with learning disabilities have difficulty planning, and they must make an extra effort to learn some planning basics in order to survive school. On the other hand, they are spontaneous, free to respond to interesting opportunities that come into their lives. When LD symptoms are recognized as signs of latent talent, people who have them are encouraged to find positive ways to express themselves.

The difference between being a loser and a winner can be as simple as changing the way we look at something. Following are some general tendencies and characteristics of people with learning disabilities.

have scattered thoughts	**but**	are curious and have many interests
daydream	**but**	can be visionaries
escape into a fantasy world	**but**	imagine new possibilities
don't think in straight lines	**but**	discover new ways of doing things
aren't motivated by others	**but**	are independent
are "troublemakers"	**but**	have leadership abilities
have low impulse control	**but**	take risks
are stubborn	**but**	are persistent

As you read the following positive traits that many people with learning disabilities possess, see if you can think of more to add to the list.

Many people who have learning disabilities

- can do more than one thing at once
- are great at functioning under pressure
- often come up with unique, clever, and new ideas
- are flexible and open minded and look at problems from new angles
- have the energy to get things done
- are nonconformists, daring to be different
- are complex thinkers

Boosting Self-Esteem and Beating Stress

Having terrific qualities doesn't mean much if a person doesn't use them. Often people with LD try so hard to fit in and think like everyone else that they stop themselves from pursuing their dreams in life. Afraid of how other people will judge their ideas, they hide the gifts that their learning disability has brought them. Some people with learning disabilities don't have very much faith in their ideas because they are convinced that they aren't as smart as other people and they are ashamed of that. They give up trying—which is the real shame, because it doesn't have to be that way.

Challenges such as learning disabilities don't hold people back. Negative attitudes held by the people facing the challenges are what keep them from living the kind of life they want. The best way to move ahead is to start feeling better about yourself. Raising your self-esteem doesn't happen overnight. It's something you need to work on every day and is just as—if not more—important than learning the parts of speech and the multiplication tables. Our self-esteem affects, not only our ability to learn, but the type of relationships and jobs we will have as well. Our self-esteem determines how happy we will be, not only with ourselves, but also with the rest of the world.

Wanda can't stop thinking about the times she's tried things and not been able to do them. She spends so much time mentally abusing herself over her difficulty with telling her right from her left that she forgets completely to think about her talents. These include being good at entertaining young children with the stories she tells—stories about monsters and knights and aliens from outer space that she makes up on her own. Gary is so down on himself for not being able to play football and not having the ability to be a mechanic that his thoughts almost never touch upon the fact that he can draw beautiful pictures or that *he* taught his parents how to use their new computer. Nathan is so focused on his forgetfulness that he overlooks his musical abilities.

People whose low self-esteem hides their talents can raise it by

• focusing on the positive when they think about themselves;

- making a conscious effort to stop negative thoughts;
- paying attention to their strengths;
- doing what they can to strengthen their weaknesses;
- taking responsibility for themselves and not blaming others;
- figuring out their feelings and talking them out instead of acting them out;
- learning to forgive themselves for making mistakes; and
- taking a break from all the self-analysis and doing something for someone else.

Our attitudes are a major factor in whether or not we perceive a situation as being stressful. Having a negative outlook about our learning disabilities can cause us unnecessary tension. The anger, denial, helplessness, and shame that come with a low sense of self-worth are all stressful emotions. For that reason, working on self-esteem issues can help people deal with stresses in their lives without overreacting to them. They know they are worthy people, and that fact doesn't change even if someone doesn't like them or they fail a quiz.

A solid sense of self-worth helps a person to move through life with a calmer attitude about what is going on around them, but even people who generally feel good about themselves have experiences that cause them anxiety. For a person with a learning disability, some of these things might be having to stand up to a teacher, hearing the put-downs and teasing that may come from insensitive people, or being transferred from a regular classroom to one for special classes. Often just coping with the day-to-day demands of school and social relationships can be more stressful for someone with LD than it is for other people.

Stress causes people to feel nervous or jumpy; they become easily startled. Sometimes people under stress act irritable. Other signs that a person is experiencing too much stress include

- lowered grades because of difficulty concentrating;
- withdrawal;
- feeling tired much of the time;
- having difficulty sleeping;
- losing one's appetite; and
- headaches and stomachaches.

People under stress experience these symptoms because stressful situations cause the body to be ready to run or to stand and fight in order to help the person survive. Although the stress response can be a good thing in an emergency, when it continues for a long period of time, it can cause health problems. When a person is aware of stress, he or she can take steps to reduce those stresses or to cope with his/her reaction to them.

A good first step to reduce stress, besides working on your self-esteem, is to look at your life and see if you are working too hard. If so, maybe you need time to spend more time relaxing by doing more of the things you like to do, activities that take your mind off your problems. Feeling that everything needs to be perfect is a setup, not only for stress, but for failure and procrastination, which also cause stress. People, with or without learning disabilities, can never be perfect, no matter how hard they try. When we stop making impossible demands on ourselves and feeling horrible when we don't meet them, then we can start setting more realistic goals and feel good about ourselves when we achieve them.

Some things people can do on their own to help them get through tough times are to

- listen to their body to be able to recognize the signs of stress;
- take a minivacation by putting on headphones and listening to music;
- strike a balance between spending time alone and with others;
- develop a sense of humor;

- get plenty of physical activity;
- eat a balanced diet, including whole grains, fruits, and vegetables;
- get enough sleep;
- be kind to themselves by nurturing with positive self-talk; and
- talk to a friend about how they are feeling.

Once in a while we hit a place in the road of life that is so rough that we can't handle it on our own. At these times our feelings of being overwhelmed are more than temporary. They pull us into a downward spiral of depression, and we feel lost, like we can't find our way again on our own. Other times we might get so angry at the person or the situation that is causing the stress in our lives that we want to hurt the people we feel responsible or do something harmful to ourselves, such as using alcohol or drugs.

At these times it is important to seek help. We can start by talking to an adult we trust. That could be a parent, a teacher, a religious counselor, or a youth worker. As we share our problems with them, we need to be honest about what we are feeling and not try to make ourselves seem stronger than we really are. Sometimes school counselors can help us through the problems that are causing us to feel stressed. Other resources that are available to offer help are mental health clinics and psychologists and psychiatrists. There is nothing wrong with getting help from others for our emotional problems. It is a brave thing to do, and it is a wise thing to do as well.

Daring to Dream: Career Choices

Because learning disabilities can make it difficult to get through the day or the week, students with LD don't think beyond today. Graduating from high school seems very far into the future. Some students with learning disabilities who have experienced a great deal of difficulty with their classes, seriously doubt that they will ever make it as far as a graduation ceremony. If they don't feel confident about their abilities and if, in the past, their teachers or parents told them their career dreams weren't realistic for someone with LD like theirs, then they might avoid deliberately thinking about the future at all.

The good news for students with learning disabilities is that there is life after high school. That life can include vocational training and even college and eventually a good job. In fact, 80 percent of college graduates diagnosed with a learning disability end up in professional or managerial jobs, according to one study. The bad news is that the future for young people who don't finish high school isn't nearly so bright. Fewer than a quarter of high school students with learning disabilities who drop out make enough money to support themselves as adults.

Never is the advice to plan ahead as critical as it is for career planning. Students with LD need to start early; ninth grade isn't too soon to make themselves familiar with their particular LD and the effects it has on both education and careers. For example, a student who has a very hard time mastering social skills and doesn't work well under pressure probably wouldn't want to be a convention planner or a youth worker. Someone who dislikes math and does poorly at it isn't going to be happy working as an accountant. At the same time, just because something is difficult for a person, doesn't mean he or she shouldn't at least try it. Often a person's determination can be just as big a success factor as the ease with which one learns a skill.

At the same time students gain awareness of the challenges that their learning disabilities may present in the world of work, they need to keep in mind their abilities and how they can best use them in that context. Some vocational counselors believe that people with learning disabilities might actually be better in some careers than people who think conventionally.

For example, people with attention deficit disorder often make very good entrepreneurs, salespeople, or detectives, or a person who has dyslexia could become an outstanding teacher. A few LD experts believe that as computers become more important, especially the Internet with its nonlinear way of presenting information, people who can handle that often illogical flow of visuals and make snap decisions will be in high demand.

Some ways to start learning how your strengths could fit into the workplace are to

- take high school electives in a number of areas to find out what interests you and what you are good at doing;
- explore interests and abilities by participating in school activities, volunteering, and working after school;
- consider the possibility of taking work-study classes that will allow you to see what a possible career is all about;
- find out about the possibility of a summer internship, an unpaid hands-on work experience;
- check out career fairs sponsored by employers, colleges, and vocational schools;
- talk to parents and adult friends about their jobs and ask if you can "shadow" them at their workplace for a day; and
- talk to your school counselor about getting vocational counseling through your school.

Students can also get ready for the future by mastering basic skills and checking out the job market to see if there really are openings in the career they think they might want to pursue. They can start finding out education require-ments before they begin working in the career area that interests them. Sometimes parents, teachers, or counselors try to discourage students with learning disabilities from choosing careers that involve education beyond high school. They may think they are doing this to protect the students from failure or for other reasons that involve the students' own good. Unfortunately, what they may be doing is limiting students' career choices and preventing them from pursuing a choice they might be very good at.

The education necessary for the career that a student is interested in pursuing might require vocational training. Private business and technical schools as well as two-year colleges provide this type of education. If a student dislikes school and doesn't want to attend two more years of classes, many schools offer certificates rather than associate of arts degrees. These usually take six to nine months to complete. In other cases, such as careers in the building trades, an apprenticeship or on-the-job training will be necessary.

Today many more people with learning disabilities are attending college than ever before, in part because many colleges and universities offer excellent programs and services specifically designed for learning disabled students. According to the HEATH Resource Center, an organization that helps college-bound students with LD, the percentage of full-time first-year students who report having a learning disability has doubled from 15 to 32 percent of all college students with disabilities since 1985.

Students planning to attend college, however, need to know that it is very different from high school. The average high school student spends more than 1,000 hours a year in class, but the average college student spends about 330 hours in class each year. On the surface, college sounds like a snap until you realize that professors assign on the average two to four times as much homework as high school teachers do. The type of homework they assign is much more complex. Instead of daily assignments given in high school, in college you are expected to less frequent, but larger ones, such as one or two major papers a semester. Most college homework consists of reading, which is important to do since professors rarely lecture from the text but ask test questions based on the material the book contains.

Students who work hard and want to go to college but aren't quite sure they can handle the extra work required can test out the plan before plunging head-first into college life. One way to do this is to sign up for a college-level class during the summer or during the last year of high school. Classes like these are called "dual-enrollment" courses. Another way of testing the waters is to ask a high school teacher to set up an independent study project or two that will resemble some of the work students might be required to do in college. A teacher can help coach them through the assignment and give valuable feedback on the skills areas that need improvement before college.

Students with LD go through the same process of college selection and preparation as do other students—with the exception of some important extras. In 10th grade it is a good idea for students with learning disabilities to begin reading through college catalogs, talking to the school counselor to gather information in order to be able to choose the right school. Because not all colleges have programs for people with LD, high schoolers may want to look for one that does offer special services. These can range from assistance finding one's way around campus and figuring out the right textbooks to buy to workshops on study skills and tutoring. Students can further prepare for college by requesting that schools reevalaute them under IDEA fairly close to the time they will graduate so that the information documenting the LD will be current when they go to post-secondary school. The new school can use the information to help design accommodations that will make the college experience a successful one.

Even though a college may not have a special program for students with learning disabilities, if it receives federal funding then it must provide reasonable accommodations for students who have LD. To receive accommodations, students must notify the school of their learning disability at the time they register and must take the responsibility to share this information with their professors at the beginning of the term or the semester. This is known as *disclosure.* Waiting until right before finals to request extra time on the test won't work. Colleges are not required to modify the courses students must take to obtain a degree, so it's a good idea, when college shopping, to see exactly what is expected. For example, if you have a terrible time with languages, find a school or a degree program that doesn't have a foreign language requirement.

You will also need to talk to your high school counselor about signing up to take the SAT (Scholastic Aptitude Test), ACT (the American College Test), or both of them. The results of these tests are often used by college admissions personnel as one of the deciding factors about who to accept. Your school counselor can help you register for the test or tests and fill out the paperwork requesting accommodations, as well as the admissions applications for the schools to which you want to apply. Students diagnosed with learning disabilities have a right to apply for accommodations, such as extra time, for these tests. To increase your chance of a high test score, it's a good idea to practice sample tests available from your counselor or to buy a practice test book and familiarize yourself with what will be expected of you before you take the test.

Even if you have low score that does not necessarily mean that you can't go to college. Not all schools pay as much attention to standardized test scores as others do. Some schools, especially many two-year colleges, have open admissions policies. If you have graduated from high school, you will be admitted even if your grades aren't the best. Sometimes you may be required to take remedial math, reading, or writing classes, which don't count toward your degree. These classes help you catch up to other students in regular classes. Even though colleges with open admissions enroll many students who otherwise couldn't get into school, the standards at these institutions of higher learning once a student is attending are usually just as high as other colleges.

Students who enter the world of work after high school face challenges too. Many are surprised to discover more rules exist in the workplace than there ever were in school. If they are even five minutes late too many times, they aren't sent to the principal's office; they are fired. The same holds true for talking back to their boss, not following the expected dress code, and not getting their work done on time in the manner they are expected to do it. Workers with learning disabilities need to

- know that there will be rules in the workplace and that they will be expected to follow them;
- understand the rules and expectations where they work;
- ask for clarification about the rules they don't understand;
- make their best effort to follow them;
- ask only if absolutely necessary that rules be changed; and
- not take it upon themselves to change the rules on their own.

As we discussed in Chapter Four, the Americans with Disabilities Act makes it illegal for employers to discriminate in hiring based on LD if the disability won't directly interfere with the job the employee is expected to do. The law also forbids discrimination in promotion. According to research from the University of Kansas, adults with learning disabilities do not report having trouble being hired. They do, however, say that once they are hired, they often remain stuck in entry-level jobs. Sometimes this is because they lack the training necessary to advance. Poor social skills may also keep them down.

Failure to be promoted simply because they have a learning disability is discrimination and illegal under the ADA. The law gives employers the responsibility to provide reasonable accommodations so that workers with disabilities, including learning disabilities, can perform their jobs. These accommodations might include a computer with a spell checking program, or they might involve permitting an employee to tape record instructions rather than writing them down. To receive accommodations, employees with LD have a responsibility to make their learning disability known and to ask for accommodations.

Despite the fact that Gary's special classes boosted his achievement levels, he still had a difficult time getting along with people—especially his family. The anger he felt toward his parents and the resentment they felt toward him held all of them back. His mother was still troubled with thoughts that her drinking during pregnancy had damaged her son. She alternated between indulging him because she felt guilty for what she had done and expressing fury when he didn't behave.

When Gary's special education teacher suggested family counseling, his parents agreed. At first the sessions were filled with blaming and anger, but the counselor suggested ways to work through the resentments, and after a month Gary began to feel better about himself and his place in the family. Now when they talked, he and his parents could sometimes express the positive feelings they had for one another instead of the loud arguments he was used to.

To make matters even better, the medication his doctor prescribed was helping him calm down to the point that he found it easier to make friends: two students from his special class and one from the regular classes he attended each afternoon. Gary still had his difficult days, but no longer did he feel like a strange visitor from another planet. People started liking him, and to his surprise, he actually began liking other people.

Between schoolwork and doing odd jobs for neighbors in order to save money for a computer of his own, he was too busy to get into trouble as he had done before. He knew he could never undo the past—those horrible years when it had seemed like the whole world was against him—but life was getting better for him, something he had never imagined could happen.

Wanda's newfound ability to read meant that she no longer had to spend so much time and energy trying to act like everyone else. Slowly, she began coming out of her shell. It helped when her tutor encouraged her to stop constantly dwelling on what she had difficulty doing and let herself enjoy activities that came easily to her.

At first Wanda couldn't think of anything she would like to do, but after she arranged the study corner in her room, she began to think that maybe she could redecorate the entire room. She saved her allowance and began going to second-hand stores looking for bargains. With occasional advice from her mother and father, she painted the walls a cheerful yellow and altered lace curtains to fit her windows. Her dad showed her how to use his power tools to make a bookcase.

Measuring all the boards was difficult at first, but Wanda discovered that she loved the smell of the sawdust and the way the pieces she'd cut fit together. After two tries, she finished her first project. Right away, she wanted to start another. With her dad's help, she built a nightstand. Before long she was going to the library to check out books so that she could find patterns for things she wanted to make and learn about how to finish the wood. Her parents were so impressed by her enthusiasm and the careful way she used the tools that they allowed her to take driver's education.

School still held little appeal for Nathan, and he doubted that it ever would. Reluctantly at first, he began looking at his career options. The school guidance counselor set up a day for him to visit the office of the pro basketball team in his city. That job shadowing experience was an eye opener, especially the part when the business manager told him that he would need at least two years of college before working for a sports organization.

All of a sudden Nathan could see that doing just enough to get by in school wasn't going to get him very far, not now that he had a goal. How to get where he wanted to be seemed confusing, but his school counselor helped him to list the small steps he would need to take in order to get into college and eventually work for a team. Grades were important as were the classes he would need to take.

One of the steps to reach his goal was to help the basketball coach at his school. At first all the details he was expected to keep track of were overwhelming, but soon he learned to write everything down. It was a matter of getting himself organized. He began feeling more optimistic about his value since in his own way, he was part of the team. The players and the coaches depended on him. Instead of spinning his wheels and going around in circles, he was going somewhere.

Whether we are at school or at home, hanging out with friends or at work, learning disabilities do not make or break us. They are only part of who we are, not the whole person. It is our attitude about ourselves and the world that really counts. Successful people make a good thing out of being different, instead of letting it stop them from living full lives. They have the will to succeed. They don't give up easily. When they need help, they are not afraid to ask for it. They have the courage to make mistakes and keep on trying. They are not afraid to work. They are people like General George Patton, Sir Isaac Newton, Whoopi Goldberg, and Woodrow Wilson. They have learning disabilities, and they make a big difference in our world.

9

Where to Find Help

Learning Disabilities

Organizations
In addition to providing general information about learning disabilities, many organizations offer help for both children and adults who struggle with the problems these disabilities cause.

Attention Deficit Information Network
475 Hillside Avenue
Needham, MA 02194
(617) 455-9895
This group helps people with ADD find solutions to practical problems they face as a consequence of ADD; as well as providing information about current research.

Children and Adults with Attention Deficit Disorders
CH.A.D.D.
8181 Professional Place, Suite 201

Landover, MD 20785
(800) 233-4050
This organization is one of the best places to turn for information about ADD. CH.A.D.D. publishes a newsletter and serves as an advocate.

HEATH Resource Center (Higher Education and Adult Training for People with Handicaps)
American Council on Education
One Dupont Circle, Suite 800
Washington, DC 20036
(800) 544-3284
This national clearinghouse provides information and help about post–high school educational options for students with learning disabilities

International Dyslexia Association
Chester Building
8600 LaSalle Road, Suite 382
Baltimore, MD 21286
(800) 222-3123
This organization provides information and referrals on testing, tutors, workshops, and conferences having to do with dyslexia.

Learning Disabilities Association of America
4156 Library Road
Pittsburgh, PA 15234
(412) 341-8077
This group provides information and referrals to state chapters, parent resources, and local support groups. It also publishes a professional journal.

Learning Disabilities Association of Canada
323 Chapel Street, No. 200
Ottawa, Ontario K1N7Z2

Canada
(613) 238-5721
This nonprofit group conducts programs through terriorital offices throughout Canada. It provides information for both LD children and adults.

National Center for Learning Disabilities
99 Park Avenue, Sixth Floor
New York, NY 10016
(212) 687-7211
A source of referrals and resources, this organization publishes *Their World* magazine, focusing on personal experiences of children and adults with dyslexia.

Resources on the Internet

Dyslexia the Gift
http: www.dyslexia.com
This site features articles on dyslexia, a forum, an events calendar, and a bookstore. It also has an extensive resource list of links to more than 100 related sites on the Internet, including many that deal with the experiences of dyslexia, even a web page designed by dyslexic teens to help other young people.

LD Online
http://www.ldonline.org
Sponsored by Washington's public television station, WETA, this Internet site is an excellent source for information, including fact sheets and both simple and in-depth articles, about learning disabilities, including attention deficit disorder. A section called KidZone features art work, stories, and articles written by children and teenagers with LD. The site also features stories about personal experiences with LD and offers a bulletin board so that people who use the site can communicate with one another. LD Online has a store offering helpful products for those with

learning disabilities and a comprehensive list of sources for help.

National Institute of Mental Health
http://www.nimh.nih.gov/publicat/learndis.htm
This site is one of the best places to look for thorough explanations of learning disabilities and to check out the latest research. It also has an extensive resource list.

Help for Related Problems

Literacy

GED Hotline (800) 629-9433
Provides information and referrals regarding getting a General Education Diploma

Literacy Volunteers of America, Inc.
635 James Street
Syracuse, NY 13203-2214
(315) 472-0001
A network of more than 375 locally based programs, LVA refer adults to literacy programs in their area.

National Adult Literacy Database, Inc.
Scovil House
703 Brunswick Street
Fredricton, New Brunswick E3B 1H8
Canada
(800) 720-NALD
NALD has information on literacy and refers people to programs throughout Canada.

Fetal Alcohol Syndrome and Birth Defects

March of Dimes National Office
Birth Defects Foundation
1275 Mamaroneck Avenue

White Plains, NY 10605
(914) 997-4722
The March of Dimes shares information about birth defects.

National Clearinghouse for Alcohol and Drug Information
PO Box 2345
Rockville, MD 20847-2345
(800) 729-6686
NCADI provides information about alcohol- and drug-related birth defects and treatment referrals.

Family Crisis Resources

National Clearinghouse on Childhood Abuse and Neglect
PO Box 1182
Washington, DC 20013
(800) 394-3366
This clearinghouse gathers and provides information on a variety of topics having to do with child abuse. It also makes referrals.

National Coalition Against Domestic Violence
PO Box 34103
Washington, DC
(202) 638-6388
This organization provides information about domestic violence and referrals to local shelters and mental health professionals who work with victims of battering.

Crisis Hot Lines for Teens

Boys Town National Hotline (800) 448-3000
Confidential Runaway Hotline (800) 231-6946
National Runaway Switchboard (800) 621-4000
National Youth Crisis Hotline (800) 442-HOPE

For Further Reading

Clayton, Lawrence, and Jaydene Morrison. *Coping with a Learning Disability*. New York: Rosen Publishing Group, 1995.

Cummings, Rhoda, Ed.D., and Gary Fisher, Ph.D. *The Survival Guide for Teenagers with LD*. Minneapolis: Free Spirit Publishing, 1990. (Also available on tape.)

Dwyer, Kathleen. *What Do You Mean I Have a Learning Disability?* New York: Walker & Comp., 1991.

Fullen, Dave. *Lessons Learned: Students with Learning Disabilities, Ages 7–9, Share What They've Learned about Life and Learning*. Columbus, Ohio: Mountain Books & Music, 1993.

Hall, David E. *Living with Learning Disabilities: A Guide for Students*. Minneapolis: Lerner Publishing Group, 1996.

Kelly, K., and P. Ramundo. *You Mean I'm Not Lazy, Stupid, or Crazy?* Cincinnati, Ohio: Tyrell & Jeremy Press, 1993.

Lewis, Erica Lee. *Help Yourself: Advice for College-Bound Students with Learning Disabilities*. New York: Random House, 1996.

Parker, R. *Making the Grade: An Adolescent's Struggle with ADD*. Plantation, Fla.: Impact Publications, 1992.

Quinn, P., and J. Stern. *Putting on the Brakes: Young People's Guide to Understanding Attention Deficit Hyperactivity Disorder*. New York: Magination Press, 1991.

INDEX